NOTHING
BEYOND THE NECESSARY

ROMAN CATHOLICISM
AND THE
ECUMENICAL FUTURE

D1300232

by
Jon Nilson

PAULIST PRESS
New York/Mahwah, N.J.

Acknowledgments

The Publisher gratefully acknowledges use of the following materials: Excerpts from "Unity of the Churches: Actual Possibility or Eschatological Actuality?" from *Philosophy and Theology*, published by Marquette University Press; excerpts from "Ecumenical Shortcuts," the translation of Daniel Ols' critique of Rahner and Fries, from *Unity of the Churches*, translated by John F. Hotchkin, Office of Ecumenical Affairs, United States Catholic Conference; excerpts from "Papal Primacy: From Obstacle to Opportunity," from *Ecumenical Trends*, October 1991 issue.

Cover design by James Brisson

Library of Congress Cataloging-in-Publication Data

Nilson, Jon.
    Nothing beyond the necessary : Roman Catholicism and the ecumenical future / Jon Nilson.
        p.   cm.
    Includes bibliographical references and index.
    ISBN 0-8091-3576-0 (alk. paper)
    1. Catholic Church—Relations. 2. Church—Unity. 3. Ecumenical movement. 4. Papacy and Christian union. 5. Ministry and Christian union. I. Title.
BX1784.N55 1995
282—dc 20   95-11964
                                                                                    CIP

Published by Paulist Press
997 Macarthur Boulevard
Mahwah, NJ 07430

Printed and bound in the
United States of America

Contents

Acknowledgments

I am very grateful to my academic home, Loyola University of Chicago, for the research leave that enabled me to write this book. I am especially grateful to my colleagues and friends in Loyola's Theology Department and to Dr. U.C. von Wahlde, Chairperson from 1987 to 1993.

The General Theological Seminary appointed me as Visiting Sabbatical Professor for Easter Term 1994. The seminarians, staff, faculty, and administration welcomed me into their community. I am particularly grateful to Bishop Craig Anderson, General's President and Dean; to Rev. Melissa Skelton, Vice-President; to Dr. William Franklin and Rev. Dr. J. Robert Wright, with whom I serve on the Anglican-Roman Catholic Consultation in the United States. Professor Wright was most responsible for my invitation to the seminary. I owe him a special debt of gratitude for that and for the years of his friendship, too.

My thanks also go to Rev. Elias Mallon, S.A., Director of the Graymoor Ecumenical and Religious Institute, for permission to use substantial portions of my article "Papal Primacy—From Obstacle to Opportunity," which first appeared in *Ecumenical Trends,* for Chapter Four; to Dr. Robert Masson, editor of *Philosophy and Theology,* for permission to use substantial portions of my article "Unity of the Churches: Actual Possibility or Eschatological Actuality?" for Chapter Two. With his permission and my gratitude, I use Rev. John F. Hotchkin's translation of Daniel Ols' "Scorciatoie ecumeniche [Ecumenical Shortcuts]" published in *L'Osservatore Romano* (25–26 February 1985), which he prepared for a "Free Conference" sponsored by Division of Theological Studies of the Lutheran Council in the U.S.A., Techny, Illinois, 16–18 April 1985.

Preface

> In ecumenical work, Catholics...[have as their] prima-
> ry duty...to make an honest and careful appraisal of
> whatever needs to be renewed and achieved in the
> Catholic household itself, in order that its life may bear
> witness more loyally and luminously to the teachings
> and ordinances which have been handed down from
> Christ through the apostles.
>
> —Vatican II, *Unitatis Redintegratio*, #4

After Vatican II, the inauguration and progress of official dialogues aimed at reuniting the Christian churches made headlines.
Surprise and delight greeted their discoveries of a genuine unity of
faith beneath the relatively superficial differences of theological
terminology. The reconciliation and reunion of Christianity that
had seemed impossible for centuries now seemed probable within a
decade.

Now, however, these dialogues seem stalled. Our time has
been called the "ecumenical winter." The hopes and enthusiasms
that sprang up in the wake of Roman Catholicism's embrace of the
ecumenical movement at Vatican II have faded. In some quarters,
they have completely died out.

Seasoned veterans of ecumenism are close to retirement.
They see few coming after them who are prepared and eager to
carry on the work. To younger theologians and church leaders,
ecumenism is very old and unexciting news. New and exciting to
them are the emergence of non-Western forms of Christianity in
the third world and dialogue with the great non-Christian religious traditions. They are also convinced that the churches' action
for justice is the most effective way to proclaim the good news
today. They have little time or interest left for ecumenism.

While Roman Catholic declarations of irrevocable commitment to the "full visible communion of all Christians [as] the ultimate goal of the ecumenical movement" (Directory, 20) continue
to be issued, its leaders still do not do all that they can do and all
that they must do to substantiate their words. If this is ecumenical
winter, Roman Catholic creativity and courage have done little to
hasten the coming of spring.

Granted, many ecumenical commitments were made and
ecumenical initiatives were undertaken during that post-conciliar
springtime of ecumenism in the late 1960s. Then buds of mutual
understanding, warmed by a fervor of optimism, were popping up
all over the ecclesiastical landscape. There were few who knew or
even suspected then how deeply entrenched were the habits of
thinking and acting that had been nurtured over the centuries of
division.

Now it seems just as easy to uproot those habits of separation as to uproot a sequoia tree. Church leaders today might
understandably feel that the hearts of the ecumenical pioneers
were in the right place but their eyes were not. Those who committed their churches to the quest for full, visible unity did not see
deeply enough to make good on their commitments. Now the real
obstacles are clear. For the moment, reconciliation is impossible
and perhaps it is even unnecessary for the foreseeable future.
Now is the time for realism, time to mute people's expectations
and hopes for a church that is vibrantly and visibly one.

Yet an official ecumenical retrenchment like this is incon-
ceivable. Can Jesus' prayer that all be one (Jn 17:21), the prayer
that has served as the summons, light, and guide of the ecumenical
movement, be impossible for God to answer? Can the solemn
commitments to full, visible unity made by the churches have had
such fragile bases that we can now revoke them without disobey-
ing the Spirit and breaking faith with our forefathers and mothers
in the church? Does the witness of millions of Christians who have
lived, worked, prayed, suffered and even died together for the love

of Jesus Christ and of each other have no meaning for us, no claim upon us?

No, the ecumenical movement *is* irreversible. The ecumenical question for us today has not faded back to "if" or "whether." It remains what it has always been: "*How*? How are we best to cooperate with the grace of the Holy Spirit in our time to restore the unity of the Church of Jesus Christ?"

This book offers a Roman Catholic answer to this question. Its title is drawn from Acts 15:28, which is quoted in Vatican II's Decree on Ecumenism, *Unitatis Redintegratio*, #18: "…this sacred synod confirms what previous councils and Roman pontiffs have proclaimed: in order to restore communion and unity or preserve them, one must 'impose no burden beyond what is indispensable [*necessaria*].' The council urgently desires that every effort should henceforth be made toward the gradual realization of this goal…."

Abbreviations

DS   Denzinger, H.J.D. and Schönmetzer, ed. *Echiridion symbolorum, definitionum et declarationum de rebus fidei et moribus.* 33rd ed. Barcelona: Herder, 1965.

FD   *Fidei Depositum*, Apostolic Constitution of Pope John Paul II.

CCC   *Catechism of the Catholic Church*

DV   *Dei Verbum*, Dogmatic Constitution on Divine Revelation, Vatican II (4 December 1963)

ARC-USA   Anglican-Roman Catholic Consultation in the United States

ARCIC   Anglican-Roman Catholic International Commission

CDF   Congregation for the Doctrine of the Faith

UR   *Unitatis Redintegratio*, Decree on Ecumenism, Vatican II (21 November 1964)

GS   *Gaudium et Spes*, Pastoral Constitution on the Church in the Modern World, Vatican II (7 December 1965)

LG   *Lumen Gentium*, Dogmatic Constitution on the Church, Vatican II (21 November 1964)

WCC   World Council of Churches

Translations from the documents of Vatican II are taken from Walter M. Abbott, and Joseph Gallagher, eds., *The Documents of Vatican II*. New York: America, 1966. Some have been modified for the sake of clarity and inclusive language.

Chapter One

CHRISTIANITY IS COALESCING

Ecumenism has been pushed further and further down on the churches' agenda because it seems to be an intolerably churchy concern. Church unity is a cause that demands too much effort and yields too few results so long as people are bleeding and starving to death on the churches' very doorsteps. Standing before the overwhelming scope of today's needs, many feel that the churches can best proclaim the gospel by imitating the good Samaritan. Ecumenical position papers and agreed statements, plus the extraordinary investment of time and money needed to produce them, seem unjustifiable in the face of human suffering. Ecumenism seems quaint at best, a dangerous distraction at worst.

Ecumenists themselves are partially to blame for this perception of their work. We have allowed ourselves to become consumed by the goals of mutual understanding and full, visible unity of the churches and have forgotten that these are not ultimate goals. We have not shown clearly enough that the unity of the churches is critical to the unity of the world.

The ecumenical goal is not unity for the sake of unity, but unity for the sake of a world that needs the churches to come together. The church, according to Vatican II, is "a kind of sacrament or sign of intimate union with God, and of the unity of all humankind...an instrument for the achievement of such union and unity" (LG, #1). Indeed, the Church's mission in and to the world can offer "a function, light, and powers which can serve to constitute and consolidate the human community according to the divine law....For the promotion of unity belongs to the innermost nature of the church" (GS, #42).

Now a church divided can still foster human community but its effectiveness is severely limited. A divided Church declares,

1

whether it wants to or not, that differences justify separation—and even competition. The church of Christ can help to constitute and consolidate the human community only insofar as it is a model of unity itself, a reconciliation of diversities wherein serious differences are discussed, marginal differences are celebrated, and all differences enrich the whole.

Another reason for the discouragement that afflicts ecumenism today, that pervading sense that this era is truly an "ecumenical winter," is the dead end that the bi-lateral dialogues seem to have reached.

Dialogue has been the Roman Catholic Church's main ecumenical strategy during and since Vatican II (Tavard, Principles, 401). Even before the council ended, the U.S. bishops had established commissions to explore the possibility of official dialogues with other church bodies. Since the council, the church has established direct dialogues on the local, national, and international levels with the other major Christian bodies, as well as dialogues in such multi-lateral structures as the World Council of Churches (Stransky, Ecumenism, 116), its Faith and Order Commission, and the Council of Churches for Britain and Ireland.

The church's predilection for dialogue is easy to understand. Genuine dialogue depends upon and embodies a fundamental equality and mutual respect among the partners. Engaging in dialogue between equals meant abandoning the notion that the only true ecumenism was the process of the separated churches returning to the "Roman obedience." Establishing dialogue with other Christian bodies was, therefore, the quickest and most concrete way that the Church could prove that the "ecumenism of return" had ended.

Dialogue was deemed the royal road to mutual knowledge and the dissolution of the factors that divided the churches. Study and discussion among their appointed experts would (and did!) reveal that certain differences, previously assumed to be "church-dividing," were not. They were matters of varying emphasis and terminology, not real differences in faith. Where real differences were found, surely the experts could find a way to overcome them.

Bi-lateral dialogues, such as the Lutheran–Roman Catholic and the Anglican–Roman Catholic, fastened upon the "agreed statement" as the vehicle for recording and publicizing their discoveries of unity in faith on matters formerly thought to be divisive. The agreed statements would be the churches' stepping-stones across the swamps of division. Each statement would show how the traditional language of one church was compatible with the faith of the other church partner. Some agreed statements would go further and express the shared faith in language that did not evoke the bitter controversies of the past. Pope John Paul II commended the Anglican–Roman Catholic International Commission (ARCIC) for adopting this approach:

> Your method has been to go behind the habit of thought and expression born and nourished in enmity and controversy, to scrutinize together the great common treasure, to clothe it in language at once traditional and expressive of an age which no longer glories in strife but seeks to come together in listening to the quiet voice of the Spirit (Welcome, 341).

The Directory for the Application of Principles and Norms on Ecumenism, issued by the Pontifical Council for Promoting Christian Unity in May 1993 to summarize and organize and update Roman Catholic ecumenical directives, continues to echo the preference for dialogue:

> Dialogue is at the heart of ecumenical cooperation and accompanies all forms of it....Ecumenical dialogue allows members of different Churches and ecclesial Communities to get to know one another, to identify matters of faith and practice which they share and points on which they differ....When differences are recognized as being a real barrier to communion, they

try to find ways to overcome them in the light of those points of faith which they already hold in common (Directory, #172).

Yet expert observers of contemporary ecumenism argue that dialogue alone is no longer the way toward church unity. Konrad Raiser, general secretary of the World Council of Churches, points to the fate of agreed statements, like the ARCIC *Final Report* and the WCC's Faith and Order Commission's 1982 document *Baptism Eucharist Ministry* (BEM; also known as the Lima Report). In these texts, the unity of faith discovered by the dialogue partners was articulated in language that did not resonate with particular ecclesial traditions, theological schools, or controversies. As a result, the *Final Report* and BEM became orphans. They were not "received" into the life of the Christian churches because the people were not familiar with their language (Future, 4). Naturally, they continued to use the terminology particular to their church, the words they found most comfortable and time-tested.

Another reason for the marginality of agreed statements is their style. They are composed by committees of theologians, who painstakingly weigh and sift each word. Non-theologians—and sometimes other theologians!—often find the results turgid and dull. Maybe those like myself who are responsible for writing these documents should attach a warning label to them:

NOTICE

THIS TEXT REQUIRES A TERMINAL DEGREE

IN THEOLOGY AND 10 YEARS OF

ECUMENICAL EXPERIENCE TO BE

COMPREHENDED.

Michael Fahey has a different image for the agreed statements: they are like planes that circle round and round the churches' airports without ever getting permission to touch down. They are not allowed to land for fear that they might have a bomb on board. An agreed statement may contain some fatal ambiguity or it may paper over some fundamental disagreement. Since church leaders can never be certain that the statements express a genuine unity of faith (Rahner, Aspects, 79–82), it seems safer just to keep them from materially affecting the church's life and thinking.

Formal dialogues and their resulting statements remain necessary, as Chapter Four will argue. It is now clear, however, that they alone cannot carry us to that full, visible unity that is the ecumenical goal. Dialogues between experts will produce only more agreed statements, which the churches will also keep at arm's length. The partner churches must begin sharing their lives with one another as much as possible. Only by thinking, acting, and praying together will they discern the values and convictions which constitute the real referent of the different words and symbols by which they express their faith. Only so will they learn how their different theologies, liturgies, and polities initiate them more deeply into the faith that unites them. Mutual familiarity is the necessary hermeneutical context for interpreting and receiving the agreed statements.

Words are crucial. In words we order and communicate the complex sets of external and internal data that we call "experience." At certain moments in our lives, we find that we must insist on certain words. Sometimes only the phrase "I love you," not "I like you" or "I am fond of you," will enable a relationship to continue. At certain moments in its life, the church has had to insist on certain particular formulae as the least inadequate verbal expressions of its experience of Jesus Christ. To know the meaning of *homoousios* and refuse to use it means exclusion from the church because *ipso facto* one does not share the church's experience.

When words become congealed into formulae or clichés, however, they become less reliable indicators of the experience and convictions of those who speak them. Phrases can be used mindlessly. People can become parrots in order to be accepted and admired, like students in Philosophy 101 who start to pepper their conversations with terms like "existentialism" and "phenomenology." People can repeat phrases long before they understand their meanings. Kindergarteners say the Pledge of Allegiance, just as a World War II veteran does, but they do not mean the same thing as he does.

The full scope of what people mean by their words is discerned only in the context of their lives. If I say to you, "I love you," but never do anything to make you happy, you will soon discover that the usual meaning of "I love you" is not what I meant when I said it to you.

Since mutual familiarity is the necessary hermeneutical context for interpreting and receiving the agreed statements, the challenge issued by the third world conference on Faith and Order, which met at Lund in Sweden in 1952, points the way forward:

> Should not our Churches ask themselves whether they are showing sufficient eagerness to enter into conversation with other Churches, and whether they should not act together in all matters except those in which deep differences of conviction compel them to act separately (Tomkins, 16)?

The Roman Catholic Church agrees: "Christians...will want to do everything together that is allowed by their faith....'In this unity in mission, which is decided principally by Christ himself, all Christians must find what already unites them before their full communion is achieved'" (Directory, #162; the quotation is from John Paul II's *Redemptor Hominis*). ARC-USA makes the point in more helpful detail:

> If, indeed, thought is dependent upon language and experience is dependent upon thought, then it is highly problematic to claim that one can distinguish the sub-

stance of faith from the culturally determined language of its expression. How does one discern the substance beneath the words save through the words? It is a mistake to assume that when one speaks of the mysteries of faith, one can refer beyond the various attempts to speak about those mysteries to the mysteries themselves as if they are simply there and available for inspection.

One way of dealing with this puzzle of doctrinal language is to accept orthopraxis as the test of orthodoxy: that is, to recognize that doctrines are expressions of the communal life of the church and that shared life may make differing doctrinal formulae intelligible and reveal them to be compatible and even identical in intent. But such an interpretation means that attempts to share life must precede or at least accompany attempts to compare doctrinal statements. It might even suggest that shared sacramental life must precede or at least accompany attempts to compare doctrines on sacraments (ARC-USA, Responses, 267).

If the official dialogues leading to agreed statements cannot bear the weight of the hopes that were placed on them and the churches are reluctant to share life with one another, as Lund challenged them to do, is this truly the ecumenical winter and are we now snowed in? Or is the movement of Christian churches into fuller communion going on right under our eyes?

It is easy to miss the real progress that is happening now. Ecumenism is no longer in the headlines, as it was in the years immediately following Vatican II. Then, too, we tend to look at macro-structures, like the World Council of Churches and the Roman Catholic Church, and see so little progress.

Yet the WCC was never intended to be some new "super church," absorbing all its member denominations into a unity based on their least common denominator (Tavard, Church, 198;

Stransky, Council, 1084–1085). Sometimes, too, the WCC seems more like the churches' battlefield than an oasis of Christian concord and cooperation. Roman Catholics do participate widely and regularly in the council's work, but their church still refuses full membership in it. The council's seventh assembly at Canberra (February 1991) seemed not so much a celebration of increasing unity but the arena where latent inter-church tensions could finally surface and boil.

If the history and struggles of the WCC are any guide, it is unrealistic to expect some future general council to forge, declare, and seal the unity of the Christian churches. Yet Christian unity is slowly emerging by coalescence. Partner churches are discovering their union in faith with one another and sealing their God-given realizations by significant structural changes.

A few instances of coalescence: Already in 1931 Anglicans and Old Catholics recognized one another as churches and established intercommunion (Bonn, 37–38). Lutherans, Orthodox, Anglicans and Roman Catholics are solemnly and irrevocably committed to the goal of full unity. In Canada, churches have worked out a common formation program to prepare people for baptism. In the summer of 1997 the Episcopal Church in its General Convention will vote on a "Concordat of Agreement" with the Evangelical Lutheran Church of America and the latter will vote on a proposal for unity with the Reformed churches of the United States. In February 1993, Lutherans heard their ecumenical partners, Orthodox and Roman Catholic, urge them to pursue these initiatives for unity.

Progress is underway in Latin America, too, where the Roman Catholic Church commands the loyalty of the majority of the population. In late 1993, the leaders of the Roman Catholic Church, the Episcopal Church, Lutherans, and Antiochene Orthodox put their signatures to a formal agreement that "deeply laments the divisions that have occurred within the church founded by Jesus Christ...." This agreement is seen to be the first of its kind in Latin America (Mexican, 163).

On November 17, 1993 the Porvoo Common Statement was published. It details the concrete steps and the doctrinal foundations for a communion of all the Anglican and Lutheran churches of northern Europe. When the proposal is ratified, the fifty million Christians of the Anglican churches of England, Ireland, Scotland, and Wales and of the Lutheran churches of Norway, Sweden, Finland, Denmark, Iceland, Lithuania, Latvia, and Estonia will be gathered into a single communion. Admission to each other's eucharist will be a matter of right, not just hospitality. Had the Porvoo Common Statement been published in 1970, it would have been the lead story in every newspaper and network news program. It is a sign of the times that only brief reports on Porvoo have appeared, even in the religious press. Yet it is one more sign that the future church of Jesus Christ fully and visibly united throughout the world is now forming like a crystal, silently and gradually and surely.

The Roman Catholic Church, however, remains ecumenically aloof and immobile. Certainly, ecumenism is high on its public agenda. It has established organs for ecumenical work at every level, from the Pontifical Council for Promoting Christian Unity in Rome down to ecumenical offices in the particular dioceses and religious orders (Directory, Chap. 2). Still, the church has not yet specified the terms by which it would enter into full communion with another church or churches. Nor has ecumenism effected any major post-conciliar changes in the church's liturgy, doctrine, or decision-making structures. Ecumenical icing has been daubed all over the Roman Catholic cake, but the cake still looks and tastes the same.

Undoubtedly, a number of important ecumenical declarations and gestures have been made by the Church in the persons of John XXIII, Paul VI and John Paul II. The following list is far from exhaustive.

In his first encyclical, John XXIII had spoken in the old pre-conciliar framework of the "ecumenism of return" (Hebblethwaite, Paul, 289). Nonetheless, he made sure that the separated Christians in the other churches were invited to the banquet of grace that, he hoped, the council would be (Hebblethwaite, Shepherd, 321). These Christians' influence on Vatican II was great (Bird, 24–33). John also established the Secretariat for Promoting Christian Unity in June 1960 and enhanced its status two years later so that it could influence the conciliar deliberations directly (Stransky, Secretariat, 182).

Paul VI was the first pope to visit the headquarters of the World Council of Churches in Geneva. Together with Michael Ramsey, then archbishop of Canterbury, he inaugurated the first Anglican-Roman Catholic International Commission in 1966 to work toward "that unity in truth, for which Christ prayed." He embraced Patriarch Athenagoras and lifted the excommunication imposed in 1054. When an Orthodox delegation visited him on the tenth anniversary of this event, he knelt to kiss the feet of its leader, Bishop Meliton.

John Paul II declared his commitment to fulfilling the mandates of Vatican II—including those on ecumenism—shortly after his election to the papacy (Hebblethwaite, John Paul, 447). Stransky, Sheerin, and Hotchkin have collected his subsequent ecumenical statements. Very recently, on March 25, 1993, he approved the new *Directory for the Application of Principles and Norms on Ecumenism*, which he had mandated to organize and codify the ecumenical policies of the church (Directory, 3).

The church maintains an extensive range of ongoing contacts and dialogues with other churches and Christian groups. The Joint Working Group of the Roman Catholic Church and the World Council of Churches has been meeting regularly since 1965 and publishes reports on relationships between the two bodies. Catholic observers attend and participate in WCC plenaries and commission meetings, the last being the Faith and Order meeting in Spain, August 1993. The church maintains formal international dialogues with the Orthodox, the Lutheran World Federation, the World Methodist Council, the World Alliance of Reformed Churches, and the Anglican Communion, among others. Many of these international dialogues have regional and national counter-parts, the most prominent and productive of which is the Lutheran–Catholic dialogue in the United States.

Still, Roman Catholic ecumenical efforts have remained at the tangential level of symbolic gestures, dialogues, and coopera-tion on projects of common interest. Its own structures and even its less authoritative teachings have hardly been affected by the accomplishments and insights of the ecumenical movement.

For instance, Rome has not indicated a willingness to re-examine the 1896 judgment of Leo XIII that Anglican orders are "absolutely null and utterly void," despite careful historical and theological arguments for reopening the case (ARC-USA, Orders). The Vatican has even maintained that the Anglican ordi-nation of women to the priesthood requires a review, if not a denial, of ARCIC I's agreements on ministry and ordination (Official, 129). Roman Catholic bishops therefore continue to reordain those Episcopalian priests whom they accept for service as Roman Catholic priests. Absolute "reordination" continues, while conditional ordination would require no change in church doctrine and the ecumenical reasons in its favor have been obvi-ous for years. More on this in Chapter Four.

In December 1991, nine years after the first Anglican–Roman Catholic International Commission's *Final Report* had been submitted to Rome, the Congregation for the Doctrine of the Faith, together with the Pontifical Council for Promoting Christian Unity, issued its official reaction to it. The CDF applauded the *Final Report* as a "significant milestone." Yet it asked for "further clarification or study" insofar as "the identity of the various state-ments [of the *Final Report*] with the faith of the Church" was seen to be lacking. In the eyes of the archbishop of Canterbury and other expert observers (Roman Catholics included), Rome seemed to be demanding theological conformity as the price which its ecu-menical partners will have to pay for reconciliation with it.

In September 1993 the second Anglican–Roman Catholic International Commission sent the requested clarifications of the agreed statements on eucharist and ministry to the Pontifical Council for Promoting Christian Unity. In March 1994, its president, Cardinal Cassidy, wrote to the co-chairs of ARCIC II to say that the clarifications had further illumined the issues and thus "no further study would seem to be required at this stage." The agreement reached has been "greatly strengthened." Yet his letter shows that the Vatican still does not concur with the commission's claim to have reached "substantial agreement" on the eucharist nor with their claim that Anglicans and Roman Catholics will recognize their own faith in the statement on ministry.

In October 1992, John Paul II introduced a new *Catechism of the Catholic Church.* He says that "GUARDING THE DEPOSIT OF FAITH IS THE MISSION WHICH THE LORD ENTRUSTED TO HIS CHURCH, and which she fulfills in every age" (Fidei, 1). The new catechism is, therefore, "a statement of the Church's faith and of catholic doctrine, attested to or illumined by Sacred Scripture, the Apostolic Tradition and the Church's Magisterium" (Fidei, 5). He proposes it as a means of ecclesial communion and a "sure norm for teaching the faith." The text also purportedly fosters ecumenism by "showing carefully the content and wondrous harmony of the catholic faith" (Fidei, 5-6).

While Vatican II's Decree on Ecumenism is cited forty-two times in the catechism, the pain and damage caused by the continuing divisions of Christianity remain in the distant background. The council's affirmation that the work of the Spirit among our Christian sisters and brothers contributes to our own edification and that we should not forget this (UR, #4) is absent. The apostolicity of the church is grounded almost exclusively in episcopal succession, not in teaching (Section 857 is an exception), effectively mitigating the apostolicity of the other Christian churches.

The "hierarchy of truths" in Catholic teaching (UR, #11) is mentioned in Sections 90 and 234 but not exploited ecumenically. The catechism rightly presents the Trinity as the fundamental mystery (234) and belief in the incarnation as "the distinctive sign of Christian faith" (463), but it does not place the other truths of faith on a scale of importance relative to these two. Instead, the repeated stress on the interconnected, organic character of these truths may prompt Roman Catholicism's ecumenical partners to ask, "Will the church now insist that we accept the entire catechism as proof that we are truly united in faith with them?"

From an historical viewpoint, the church's ecumenical aloofness and immobility make sense. The few, sporadic ecumenical initiatives in the Roman church prior to Vatican II do not negate Stransky's judgment:

> ... [the] Decree on Ecumenism did not affirm an already developed, sanctioned ecclesiology and practice present in the pre-Vatican II scene. The decree began a new tradition. Bishops, priests, and laity were suddenly expected to 'own' the decree and to carry out its theological, pastoral and missionary demands. Too much came too soon for too many" (Ecumenism, 115).

The decree, promulgated November 21, 1964, did include a mandate for the renewal of seminary curricula along ecumenical lines (UR, #10). Nonetheless, the men ordained before 1970 have had little or no formal education in ecumenism—and these have been the leaders of the church in the post-conciliar era.

Recall too that the Roman Catholic Church had been traumatized by the sixteenth century's reformation and what its leadership took to be its logical consequences: the sundering of the faith–reason synthesis by Galileo with empirical method and by Descartes with the *Cogito* freed from religious authority; the split between religious and political authority in the bloody French revolution; modernity's cult of progress and its Molochs of fascism and communism. As the church read history, Europe made Luther's revolt its own and wound up with Hitler and Stalin. While she waited for Europe to come to its senses, she built a Roman Catholic counter-culture and fostered a nostalgia for *The Thirteenth, greatest of centuries* (Walsh).

In 1886, the bishops of the Protestant Episcopal Church in the United States stated that "Christian unity...can be restored only by the return of all Christian communions to the principles of unity exemplified by the undivided Catholic Church during the first ages." They specified those principles in four points and declared their willingness to work toward Christian unity with any or all Christian groups. Two years later, the bishops of the Anglican Communion worldwide made substantially those same principles and aims their own, bequeathing to Christianity the Chicago-Lambeth Quadrilateral (Wright, Heritage, 14–16).

By contrast, however, when Pius XII died in 1959, the only ecumenism that the Roman Catholic Church could envision was the "ecumenism of return." All the other churches that called themselves Christian had broken their unity with the one, true church of Jesus Christ, which Pius had declared to be co-termi-nous with the Roman Catholic Church in his 1943 encyclical on the mystical body of Christ. Its unity had never been lost. Those who desired Christian unity could obtain it only by returning to Rome.

Now, nearly thirty years after the council, it is clear that the Roman Catholic Church is damaged and hampered so long as Christianity remains divided. The council itself made this point gently when it said that in the situation of a divided Christianity, "the Church herself finds it more difficult to express in actual life her full Catholicity in all its aspects" (UR, #4). In its May 1992 letter to the bishops of the Roman Catholic Church on "Some Aspects of the Church Understood as Communion," the Congregation for the Doctrine of the Faith makes the point more forcefully. Churches out of communion with Rome are described as "wounded" ("*vulnere* afficitur") since the Petrine ministry is integral to the reality of each local church (111). Yet, the letter continues, the Catholic Church too sustains a "wound" ("vul-nus...iniungitur") by the continuing divisions. (Unfortunately, the Vatican's own English translation says that the Catholic Church is "injured," not wounded, by our divisions. This mistranslation made the letter appear to deny a parity in the damage that all the churches suffer by our divisons. The Latin text, however, affirms and even emphasizes parity.)

Since Roman Catholic leaders have no accountability to other churches that have broader participatory forms of church life, they feel less urgency to establish structures of governance that would empower the laity whose dignity and responsibilities were acknowledged by the council. Non-ordained Roman Catholics participate in church decision-making only by consultation or delegation. All the decision-makers are ordained—whether the pope in the worldwide church, the bishop in his diocese, or the pastor in his parish—and they are not obliged to follow any clear directives that may emerge from consultation. While a few non-ordained Roman Catholics may exercise power in the church by specific delegation from an ordained leader, all others are constitutionally powerless.

Thus, says Orsy,

> Ever since the promulgation of the new Code of Canon Law in 1983, our church has been operating on an innovative principle: persons who have not received orders cannot genuinely participate in (take part in, be included in) the sacred operations of the church; at the most, they can "cooperate." (This is law, not doctrine.) Never before in history has there been such a sharp line drawn between clergy and laity. This juridical stance is inspired by, and based on, a theology that sees the proper and exclusive role of the laity in the sanctification of the secular world, of the temporal order. (sic) That it is a part of their vocation cannot be doubted. That it is all their vocation cannot be admitted.... To give greater role to qualified lay persons would certainly attract the attention of several Christian communities which have a high esteem for the baptismal grace and grant far more responsibility to the laity than we do (8/112).

Excepting leadership positions in religious orders, the papacy is the only elective office in the church. The pope is elected by cardinals, but the cardinals are appointed. Other decision-makers are appointed, too; most bishops are named by the pope and pastors are named by the bishop. Consultations may take place before an appointment is made, but their results do not bind those with power. So a Roman Catholic bishop is the choice of the pope, not the choice of those whom he will serve (Colella, 98–103). Likewise, a pastor is the choice of the bishop, not of those whose lives he shares.

Yet the Roman Catholic people do vote—with their checkbooks. On that account, the Roman Catholic leadership in the United States is not winning their support. Surveys show that Catholics donate a lower percentage of their income to their church than do their Christian sisters and brothers. Analysts point to Catholics' discontent with their leadership as the reason: "…the decline in Catholic contributions over the last quarter century is the result of a failure in leadership and an alienation of membership…from support of the ecclesiastical institution" (Greeley and McManus, 3-4.) Whether the U.S. bishops' recent pastoral letter on stewardship will reverse this trend remains to be seen.

The Roman Catholic Church is also weakened by its members' lack of familiarity with forms of preaching and prayer that they might find more nourishing than the ones they find solely within the Roman Catholic orbit. In the wake of Vatican II, "unliturgical" Catholic devotions gradually died out. Many Catholics were left only with the eucharist to sustain their spirituality. They had little guidance in other forms of public and private prayer that deepen the eucharistic experience.

The Anglican Communion has its Book of Common Prayer that offers the riches of the Bible and tradition to nourish public and private prayer throughout the day. (The BCP also allows for lay leaders of its public prayer.) Recently, the Presbyterian Church in the United States adopted its own prayer book, like the BCP.

Roman Catholics' spirituality could be deepened and secured on a more biblical foundation if they could know and use the BCP.

The Roman Catholic Church is also weakened by maintaining celibacy as a condition for priestly and episcopal ministry. In a church reunited, celibacy could not and would not be a requirement. Priests sustained by marriage and family relationships would celebrate the eucharist for Catholics who are now deprived of it too often in too many places. Celibacy as God's gift to an individual for the church may well be reinvigorated, too. Instead of being the painful price one must pay (more or less willingly) to be a priest, celibacy would again be a sign that "God alone suffices."

A reunited church would actualize papal primacy and infallibility more accurately and faithfully. Without critiques and corrections from our separated sisters and brothers, it is too easy for Catholics to overestimate the role of the church's teaching office.

For example, in assessing the current proposals for union between the Episcopal Church and the Evangelical Lutheran Church of America, DiNoia worries about the proposals' lack of "...institutional structures to insure its [the new union's] fidelity to the gift of truth it has received" (18). What is lacking, in his view, is the teaching authority of pope and bishops as a guarantee of the church's fidelity to the truth. While he is aware of the many other means by which revealed truth is received, assimilated, and passed on, there is only one that stands as guarantee of the Church's fidelity, the magisterium.

This position fails to reflect the proper balance among the means by which the church receives and proclaims God's gift of truth. Here scripture, tradition, theological consensus, and the lived experience of the faithful down through the ages are all rendered secondary. Vatican II, however, says,

> It is clear, therefore, that sacred tradition, sacred
> Scripture, and the teaching authority of the Church,
> in accord with God's most wise design, are so linked
> and joined together that one cannot stand without the

others, and that all together and each in its own way
under the action of the one Holy Spirit contribute
effectively to the salvation of souls (DV, #10).

The 1968 encyclical *Humanae Vitae*, to which DiNoia
alludes, gives rise to an example of the results of this imbalance.
It is no secret that most Roman Catholic theologians do not agree
with the reasons for the judgment that articifical contraception
is "*intrinsice inhonestum.*" It is also no secret that the percentage
of Roman Catholic married couples who practice articifical
contraception is the same as that for non-Catholics. Yet the
consensus of theologians counts for nothing in this matter nor
does the experience of faithful married couples. Here only the
voice of the pope counts.

Inter Insigniores, the 1976 declaration of the Congregation
for the Doctrine of the Faith, sets forth the reasons why the church
does not consider itself permitted to admit women to priestly ordination. It has been consistently and severely criticized for its weak
arguments (Stuhlmueller, Swidler). Yet it continues to stand as if it
stated the definitive Roman Catholic position. Counter-arguments
from scripture and theology are not entertained, apparently
because the CDF has spoken in 1976. Thus, the church appears
intransigent at best and unfaithful at worst. Its refusal to respond to
prima facie solid arguments against the position seems dishonest.
The determination to act as if only one authority counts in the
church and to ignore all the others which Christians have heard
and heeded for centuries seems ideologically driven.

Pace DiNoia, the magisterium is not the guarantee of the
church's fidelity. To claim that "The strongest defense against the
ideological captivity of the Church is an institutionalized form of
reflection that continually calls its membership and its leadership
to faithfulness and obedience..." (19) overlooks the humanity of
those who occupy the teaching office. Grace does not make them
sinless or omniscient. As Rahner pointed out long ago in "What is
a Dogmatic Statement?" even the most authoritative declarations

of the magisterium can be flawed by the sinfulness and ignorance that affected their formulation: "...one cannot brush aside the question as to whether dogmatic statements do not also bear the signature of guilty man..." (Rahner, Statement, 45). According to Roman Catholic teaching, there are persons empowered to teach the faith of the church authoritatively and definitively in moments of grave threat to the integrity of the gospel. There is no guarantee, according to Roman Catholic teaching, that they will always exercise this power in the most timely, intellectually responsible, and pastorally wise ways.

Kasper has it exactly right: both the Protestant and the Roman Catholic traditions know that "the truth of the gospel prevails again and again in the church...that they made use of ecclesiastical offices in this process, but both also know that these offices are no guarantee of the unadulterated transmission of the Gospel" (34). Office is but one of the means by which the guarantee of God is made good in the church. A united Christian church would live this more clearly.

Only the full visible unity of the Christian churches can furnish structure and sustenance for a society of human beings made in God's own image and likeness. Until and unless we Catholics can celebrate the eucharist with other Christians, our witness and work for justice for all is weakened. As John Paul II himself said shortly after his election, "These divisions are...an intolerable scandal, hindering the proclamation of the good news of salvation given in Jesus Christ, and the announcement of this great hope of liberation which the world needs so much today" (Address, 1).

The same unity is necessary for the Roman Catholic Church to realize its own potential more fully; to reform what needs to be reformed in its teachings, polity, and policies; to proclaim and to reflect the good news of Jesus Christ more convincingly to a world that hungers for it.

It is time and past time for the Roman Catholic Church to back up its ecumenical words by action.

Chapter Two

UNITY IS AN ACTUAL POSSIBILITY

One of the last texts Karl Rahner composed before his death on March 30, 1984 was his "Prayer for the Reunion of All Christians" (Fries, Einigung, 157–158). This text turns his convictions into petitions:

> Make the leaders of the churches clearsighted and courageous so that they feel more of a responsibility to the unity of the churches in the future than to the independence of their churches in the past. Make them daring because in the history of the Church something that is really new and great arises only when it is not competely legitimized by the past alone. Give them the joyous conviction that much more from the past can be gathered into the One Church by all the churches than is thought possible by a vision made shortsighted and fearful by the fact that what is to be gathered in was once the cause of division (Rahner, Prayers, 164–165).

One of his last books reflects these concerns, *Unity of the Churches. An Actual Possibility*, co-authored with Heinrich Fries. The radicality of their proposal, plus Rahner's reputation as the most influential Roman Catholic theologian of his generation, guaranteed that the book would get considerable attention.

They argue insistently against the cautious voices that keep muttering, "The time is not ripe yet" (2–6) because unity is a present possibility: "what is necessary is today also *actually possible*" (6). Not only is the unity of the churches "the commandment of the Lord" (1, 4), but it is also necessary for the survival of Christianity today. The plausibility of the gospel is no longer taken for granted in a secular culture. It is opposed by vigorous atheism and skepticism (1, 4). The good news is less credible to the extent that it is proclaimed by a "splintered and ruptured" multitude of churches that call themselves Christian. Moreover, these churches on their own cannot meet Christianity's responsibilities in the face of the magnitude and complexity of today's problems. The resources, expertise, and experience of all the churches together are needed to make Christian love fully effective against poverty, violence, and injustice (109–110).

Providentially, the unity that is urgent today is possible now: "But we are convinced—and to that extent optimistic—that there is an objective possibility today for creating a satisfactory and speedy church unity" (10). It lies within our reach if we see it as truly a commandment from Jesus and if we are courageous enough to set aside even some significant scruples (7). *Unity of the Churches. An Actual Possibility* identifies "the actual conditions which can already be satisfied to achieve such a possibility" (139).

Naturally, the Rahner–Fries book galvanized the ecumenical world when it first appeared. Herder put out a special edition two years later, in which Fries surveyed and responded to the main appreciations and critiques. The Division of Theological Studies of the Lutheran Council in the U.S.A. devoted a "Free Conference" (where theologians speak in their own names, not as representatives of their churches) to the book at Techny, Illinois, April 16–18, 1985. Rahner had died March 30, 1984 but Fries himself was able to attend this meeting.

After 1985, however, the excitement died down. *Unity of the Churches* seemed to take its place among all the other ecumenical texts and papers that have been consigned to the ghostly silence of the research library. Apparently, the Rahner–Fries proposal is dead. Or is it, like the daughter of Jairus, just sleeping?

It is up to the leaders and theologians of non-Roman Catholic Christian churches to decide whether the Rahner–Fries initiative is still viable, whether it succeeds in identifying a unity of faith heretofore unrealized, whether it describes a communion within which they might find themselves—surprisingly—at last reunited with the Roman Catholic Church after the separation of centuries. This chapter focuses only upon the main Roman Catholic reactions to the Rahner–Fries proposal. If it can be shown that the authors are right and that, notwithstanding the criticisms of their work, "there is an objective possibility today for creating a satisfactory and speedy church unity" (10), then practical steps toward the achievement of full, visible unity constitute a serious obligation for those who lead the Roman Catholic Church.

A Summary of Their Argument

What is the doctrinal minimum required for the unity of the Christian churches? By consensus of both its proponents (e.g. Fries, Thesis II, 3) and opponents (e.g. Ratzinger, Luther, 130–133), this is the cornerstone of the Rahner–Fries argument that the necessary conditions exist now.

Their first thesis states that "The fundamental truths of Christianity, as they are expressed in Holy Scripture, in the Apostles' Creed, and in that of Nicaea and Constantinople, are binding on all partner churches of the one Church to be" (7, 13). Christian faith is not just blind trust or vague religiosity. It has a definite content which the individual receives from the community of faith. A genuine unity of the churches must, therefore, be founded upon a true unity of faith.

The second thesis, which is Rahner's (Fries, Thesis II, 1), builds on the first:

> Beyond that, a realistic principle of faith should apply: Nothing may be rejected decisively and confessionally in one partner church which is binding dogma in another partner church. Furthermore, beyond [the content specified in] Thesis I no explicit and positive confession in one partner church is imposed as dogma obligatory for another partner church. This is left to a broader consensus in the future. This applies especially to

authentic but undefined doctrinal decrees of the Roman church, particularly with regard to ethical questions. According to this principle only that would be done which is already practice in every church today (7, 25).

Rahner takes the scriptures and the two creeds as the necessary and sufficient doctrinal basis for a genuine unity of faith. Because he does not consider the particular doctrines of the "partner churches" (*Teilkirchen*) as church-dividing, he proposes an agreement among the uniting churches. No partner church will condemn the "binding dogmas" of another partner church nor will a church make acceptance of its own dogmas a condition for unity. A church's adherence to the scriptures and creeds is enough to assure its partner churches that an authentic unity of faith exists among them.

Rahner offers three main reasons to support Thesis II. First, the scriptures and the creeds are clearly sufficient because unity *within* each church is not now secured and verified by any further explicit and detailed doctrinal agreements. Are not Catholics admitted to the eucharist every Sunday without presenting their recently signed oaths of fidelity? Do not some who publicly disagree with authoritative positions of the Church (e.g. Hans Küng, Charles Curran) still preside at the eucharist, the sign and celebration of unity? Rahner maintains that the churches must not demand more of other churches than they do of their own members. In the ordinary practice of the churches, adherence to the scriptures and the creeds, along with a common life shaped by liturgy and governance, is sufficient evidence of the unity of faith (34–36).

Rahner's second reason is that withholding assent to a true proposition is not tantamount to doubting or denying it in the intellectually complex, pluralistic situation we live in today. Withholding assent is justified when the content of the proposition has little bearing on one's own life, when the conceptual framework it presupposes is largely foreign to one's own, or when the effort to understand it is proportionately too great. Dogmatic propositions, formulated by specialists in particular historical circumstances to protect elements of the content of revelation that were then threatened, may now be existentially irrelevant for average Catholics. Ask some who are not theologians to explain their views of infallibility as defined in *Pastor Aeternus* at Vatican I and see for yourself!

The same factors hold true for social groups and churches, according to Rahner. For instance, the dogma of the Immaculate Conception will probably never be theologically important and devotionally influential for Presbyterians and Baptists, nor need it be. There are many other individual and corporate "hierarchies of truth" which co-exist peacefully with the official ones in each Christian communion (34).

The contemporary "knowledge explosion" has left its mark on Christian life. Theology has grown so vast and complex that no single individual can master it: "today's irreducible pluralism ...today's body of knowledge...can no longer be surveyed or mastered by a single individual" (28). Bernard Lonergan's essay, "Theology in Its New Context," describes a theology become empirical so that there are no omnicompetent theologians today. In every specialization besides our own, we are untutored. Even if one spends years studying Barth or Bultmann (or Rahner!), can one have any more than moral certitude that one understands him (Unity, 30; Pluralism, 9)? How much more difficult it is to be certain that the doctrines of another Christian tradition are "church-dividing" such that they indubitably constitute an obstacle to unity. The situation of faith in our churches today demands humility and tolerance.

Yet, Rahner points out, the churches actually do exercise this humility and tolerance toward their own members. They do not demand explicit and public adherence to each of their authoritative teachings from each of their members. So long as I do not abandon or oppose these teachings, or, to state it positively, so long as I share life, law, and worship with my fellow Catholics, the church recognizes me and accepts me as its own (34–36).

Rahner's third reason is that Theses 1 and 2 set forth the only basis on which the unity of the churches is realistically conceivable in our socio-cultural situation. The only unity achievable today is a unity of faith secured by adherence to the scriptures and the creeds which reserves the other disputed doctrines of the partner churches to further discussion in hopes of eventual agreement on these, too. If we do not build unity on this foundation, let us at least be honest enough to declare that our unity, which is the desire of Jesus and the condition for the survival of Christianity, is impossible (38–39).

Ols' Attack

L'Osservatore Romano is the newspaper that is taken to convey the clear but non-official views of the "highest levels" of the Vatican. So when a critique of the Rahner-Fries book by Daniel Ols entitled "Ecumenical Shortcuts" appeared on *L'Osservatore Romano*'s front page for February 25–26, 1985, it got *Time*'s attention. The newsmagazine reported Ols to have said that his piece was written at the behest of "the hierarchy," which *Time* understood as people close to the pope or even the pope himself (59).

Ols is out to demolish the Rahner-Fries proposal. He claims that the notion of truth plays no role in their work; instead, their book constitutes an argument for a real and profound overturn of the Roman Catholic faith (1). If these two authors were theological nobodies, *Unity* could be safely ignored. As it is, the reputations of Rahner and Fries make denunciation a duty (2).

Ols focuses his attack primarily on Theses I and II; in these lie the root difficulties that vitiate Theses III-VIII (9). Thesis I locates the "fundamental truths of Christianity" in the scriptures, the Apostles' Creed, and the creeds of Nicaea and Constantinople. The partner churches' adherence to these is supposed to constitute proof of a unity in faith that is sufficient to ground their ecclesial unity.

For Ols, however, the doctrines developed and defined after 381 A.D are explications of those "fundamental truths of Christianity." So the doctrinal disagreements beyond the scriptures and creeds which still divide the churches are proof that the churches are not united in faith. If you do not accept a doctrine that is a divinely-guaranteed explication of the "fundamental truths," neither do you truly accept what it explicates. The fundamentals and the explications of the fundamentals are inextricably linked (5).

Ols rejects Rahner's Thesis II as well because he denies that epistemological tolerance exists in the church. Faith is not primarily the acceptance of revealed truths; it is the acceptance of God who reveals. Only secondarily is it the acceptance of all that the church proposes as revealed by God. So one cannot accept one doctrine and withhold assent from another doctrine because the motive and reason for accepting both is the same: the authority of the revealing God (6). This is why Ols insists that the book is really a proposal for subverting the Catholic faith (1). The truths of faith all belong on the same level because one and the same authority stands behind them all, God. Ols here reflects the 1928 anti-ecumenical position of Pius XI in *Mortalium Animos* (Kasper, 26).

Ols knows that not every believer has a perfectly explicit faith. Yet authentic believers intend and desire to accept all that the church presents as divinely revealed, even if they are not explicitly aware of all of them nor quite sure of their meaning (7). Thus, Ols denies the validity of Rahner's distinction between denying a truth and withholding assent from it (7). If the church tells me that these truths are revealed by God, what grounds have I to withhold my assent and in effect to deny the authority of God to demand my assent? Ols must therefore wonder why the pope did not excommunicate Hans Küng for denying the doctrine of infallibility and why he can still celebrate the eucharist, the sign and instrument of the church's unity.

While Ols is right to characterize doctrines as explications of the fundamental content of the faith, he does not reflect on the fact that this is not always clear to the average believer—and maybe not even to the theological specialist. The philosophical presuppositions of certain doctrines (e.g. the Aristotelian notions of substance and accident) and the terminology used in their formulation are no longer familiar to many today. As the Congregation for the Doctrine of the Faith's "Declaration in Defense of the Catholic Doctrine Against Certain Errors of the Present Day [*Mysterium Ecclesiae*]" (June 1973) points out,

> The transmission of divine Revelation by the Church encounters difficulties of various kinds...the meaning of the pronouncements of faith depends partly upon the expressive power of the language used at a certain point in time and in particular circumstances...it sometimes happens that some dogmatic truth is first expressed incompletely... (110).

Thus, says the Congregation, it falls to "theologians [to] seek to define exactly the intention of teaching proper to the various formulas, and in carrying out this work they are of considerable assistance to the living magisterium of the Church, to which they remain subordinated" (111).

In his "What Is a Dogmatic Statement?" Rahner argues that the grace of God, which supports the process of developing a particular doctrine, is no guarantee that its formulation will be the clearest and fullest expression possible of the saving truth it conveys. The possibility and even likelihood always remains that sinfulness and ignorance may have influenced the way in which truths of faith are expressed. Then the crucial connection of the doctrine with the "fundamental truths" may be even more obscure. (Chapter Four will argue that the doctrine of papal primacy defined in Vatican I's *Pastor Aeternus* [1870] was affected in precisely this way.) When the unmasterable amount of data that distinguishes our age of cultural and intellectual pluralism is factored into the situation, it is clear that no one today can have a perfectly explicit faith.

Although he does not name it, Ols' argument relies on the distinction between *fides quae* (the content of faith) and *fides qua* (the trust by which we accept the content that exceeds our powers of comprehension and verification). The distinction is less useful in an age that summons us to take personal responsibility for our beliefs and convictions. Revelation's content has to bespeak its revealer. If that content is presented in language from another epoch with a philosophical framework that no longer commands agreement nor articulates a contemporary *Weltanschauung*, doctrines may seem naive, outdated, or even nonsensical—not what a loving and truthful God wants to share with those whom God loves. Rahner provides an example in his book on the Trinity. The classical trinitarian doctrine speaks of three persons in one God. If, however, I accept this teaching with a contemporary view of person as an independent center of consciousness, then I accept a heresy.

Ols does not envision the situation where the linguistic clothing of a revealed truth makes it seem so incongruous with the revealer that one must withhold one's assent for conscience's sake. Yet "Credo quia absurdum" (I believe because it is absurd) does not represent the Catholic view of faith, as the teaching of Vatican I's *Dei Filius* makes clear. Responsible believers are not delivered from uncertainties. There may be times when their fidelity to God requires them to withhold assent to a doctrine until its saving meaning can be discerned.

Nor does Ols' critique address the complexities involved in the church's being "truly and intimately linked with humankind and its history" (GS, 1). The church does not speak some supra-temporal Esperanto, but the particular languages of the cultures and eras within which it dwells. The church also penetrates more and more deeply the truths given by God (DV, #8). What it truly teaches as divinely revealed cannot simply be read out of a reference book, but must be discovered and appropriated again and again. Why else would LG, #25 speak of the duty incumbent upon even the pope to inquire diligently into the deposit of revelation? Why else would the CDF underline the importance of theological research "to define exactly the intention of teaching proper to the various formulas..." (111).

Ols proposes other unusual notions, such as the lack of any real distinction between dogmas and the deposit of faith (8), the simple identity of the church of Nicaea with the church of Trent (8), and (most tellingly) the "ecumenism of return" which maintains that ecumenism "consists in bringing others to participate fully in this fulness [of which the Catholic Church is the bearer]" (11). His perspective is neo-scholastic: strong logic, weak epistemology, no historical sense. He caricatures what he cannot refute and leaves the Rahner proposal intact. There may be legitimate concerns about the Rahner proposal, but Ols' reactions are not among them. (For Fries' own response to Ols, see his "Thesen.")

Aidan Nichols defends Rahner and Fries against Ols' charges. He even provides additional support for *Unity of the Churches* by observing that "It has to be admitted that the principles on which the Church admits to limited communion other Christian bodies (specifically, the eastern Orthodox) are far from clear...the extension of limited inter-communion to the Orthodox is not prima facie explicable if formal assent to all Catholic dogmas is a pre-condition of Eucharistic sharing" (159).

Still, he vigorously rejects their proposal because "...its pastoral imprudence is so great as to constitute a kind of practical irresponsibility vis-à-vis Catholic doctrine" (166). Yet all he offers to support this charge are two paragraphs of counter-assertions, like "The events of the *post-concilio* have demonstrated that even in a Church with as firm and long-standing a doctrinal tradition as the Catholic church, the latent possibilities of collapse into doctrinal anarchy are ever-present" (161). This is too impressionistic to refute the Rahner–Fries proposal.

Dulles' Critique

Avery Dulles offers a more instructive dissent. For him, the unity of the churches is not an actual possibility. It is not even close to realization: "We have no antecedent certainty that we shall reach the ultimate goal...before the end of historical time" (Paths, 47). Indeed, "a universal communion among all Christians as a single family of believers is an ideal which, no doubt, will never be realized within history..." (Strategies, 189). Dulles points to the "hard questions," "thorny issues," "hardcore differences," and "hidden disagreements within the previous agreements" that have emerged since the "honeymoon days" of ecumenism in the 1960s (Ecumenism, 22–23). And the Rahner–Fries proposal? It is "excessively reductionistic" (Ecumenism, 24).

"We sit on the shoulders of giants," as Bernard of Chartes reminds us. (Actually, "Dicebat Bernardus Carnotensis nos esse quasi nanos gigantium humeris insidentes ut possimus plura eis et remotiora videre, non utique proprii visus acumine aut eminentia corporis, sed quia in altum subvehimur et extollimur magnitudine gigantea," according to John of Salisbury in his *Metalogicon* III, 4. I am grateful to my friend and colleague Willemien Otten for this reference.) Now the shoulders of Rahner and Dulles are quite strong, since many of us have been sitting there for a long time! No wonder, then, that their disagreement is instructive.

Though their disagreement is substantial, the range of their agreement is extensive. They even use the same genre, theses with commentaries appended, to delineate the essentials of their position.

Dulles agrees with Rahner that a genuine unity of faith already exists between the churches and that this unity is manifested in their adherence to the scriptures, the Apostles' Creed, and the creeds of Nicaea and Constantinople. Both also affirm that the churches could be doing much more for the sake of unity than they are now. Chapter II of the Decree on Ecumenism stresses personal conversion and ecclesistical renewal as fundamental to ecumenism, but neither one considers these agenda anywhere near completion (Ecumenism, 24–25; Unity throughout). Neither one confuses church unity with uniformity; the united church of the future will and must be appropriately pluralistic.

They both underscore the ecumenical importance of UR, #11 on the "hierarchy of truths" (Unity, 20; Paths, 35). They agree that complete doctrinal agreement among the churches is probably impossible but that it is also unnecessary for reunion. Therefore, the churches should determine and declare their ecumenical "bottom lines," what each deems indispensable for full, visible unity of faith. Dulles says, *"...the churches should insist only on the doctrinal minimum required for a mature and authentic Christian faith, and that doctrines formulated in response to past historical crises should be carefully reviewed to see whether they must be imposed as tests of orthodoxy today"* (Paths, 41). Rahner's formulation is broader: "...one should finally determine more exactly, more concretely ...those conditions under which each existing church considers a speedy unity possible" (Unity, 9).

What, then, is the doctrinal minimum required for reunion? This is the critical issue that separates Rahner and Dulles.

Recall Rahner's first thesis: "The fundamental truths of Christianity, as they are expressed in Holy Scripture, in the Apostles' Creed, and in that of Nicaea and Constantinople, are binding on all partner churches of the one Church to be" (7, 13) because Christian faith is not mere trust or bland religiosity. The unity of the churches must be built on an authentic unity of faith. Dulles agrees and even cites Unity approvingly on this point. His first thesis maintains that *"...for church unity a measure of doctrinal accord is a prerequisite"* (Paths, 32).

Recall Rahner's second thesis:

Nothing may be rejected decisively and confessionally in one partner church which is binding dogma in another partner church. Furthermore, beyond [the content specified in] Thesis I no explicit and positive confession in one partner church is imposed as dogma obligatory for another partner church. This is left to a broader consensus in the future.... According to this principle only that would be done which is already practice in every church today (7, 25).

In Dulles' second thesis, he agrees that *"...complete agreement on all matters of doctrine is unattainable and ought not to be regarded as necessary"* (Paths, 32). He sketches the development of the notion of the "fundamental articles" of faith and its formulation at Vatican II under the rubric of the "order or 'hierarchy' of the truths of Catholic doctrine." He recapitulates this discussion in his third thesis, which affirms the existence of this hierarchy. He recognizes that agreements on the essentials among Christians are "more significant than their disagreements" (Paths, 35).

Dulles' fourth thesis develops the implications of his first three: *"...where there is agreement in the basic essentials of the Christian faith, and the practice of valid baptism, a considerable measure of ecclesial communion exists...." (Paths, 36)*. His fifth thesis, *"...in the Scriptures and the ancient creeds (especially the Apostles' Creed and the Nicene-Constantinopolitan Creed), the mainline churches, whether Orthodox, Roman Catholic, Anglican, or Protestant, already share in common a large fund of doctrinal materials"* (Paths, 36), seems to put him right in Rahner's camp .

Note, however, how Dulles keeps his distance. Rahner takes the scriptures and the creeds as the necessary and sufficient doctrinal basis for a genuine unity of faith. The scriptures and creeds are enough to assure each partner church that an authentic unity of faith exists among them. For Dulles, on the other hand, the creeds and scriptures are necessary but insufficient. This "large fund of doctrinal materials" is not large enough. The procession of the Holy Spirit still divides east from west, while the papal and Marian dogmas (among others) still divide the churches of the west. To be sure, whenever we find agreement in the basic essentials of the Christian faith and the practice of valid baptism, a considerable measure of ecclesial communion exists, but this considerable measure is still far short of the doctrinal agreement necessary for full, visible unity.

The three main considerations Rahner offers to support

Thesis II were outlined above: first, unity *within* each church is already maintained simply by the scriptures, the creeds, and life together in worship under common governance (34–36); second, withholding assent to a proposition is not equivalent to doubting or denying it in today's pluralistic situation; third, Theses 1 and 2 articulate the only basis for a realistically conceivable unity of the churches (38–39).

Now Dulles' sixth thesis seems parallel to Rahner's second: *"The different churches can come into closer communion if they recognize that one another's binding doctrines are, even if not true [sic!], at least not manifestly repugnant to the revelation given in Christ"* (Paths, 39). Yet this joint recognition is not the basis for full communion, but only closer communion.

To Dulles, the Rahner proposal would result in cultural, religious, and theological disaster. Drawing on his ecumenical experience, he feels that the Roman Catholic Church could refrain from condemning the central doctrines of other Christian churches as contrary to the gospel, but he doubts that certain Protestant churches could reciprocate (Paths, 37–38, Strategies, 188–189). His more substantive reason for rejecting Rahner's thesis is that he identifies withholding assent to a dogma with doubting or even denying the dogma:

> If Orthodox and Protestant Christians could come into full communion with Rome without positively affirming the modern Catholic dogmas [for example, Anglicans who *withheld assent* to the dogma of papal primacy without a Catholic commitment to reform in its manner of exercise], it would seem that Catholics could not be denied Communion in their own church if they voiced the same *doubts or denials*" (Paths 39; emphases added).

This innovation would tell Catholics and other Christians that some doctrines are dispensable for the fullness of Christian life. If you want to believe them, well and good, but if you do not, no problem. In the united church, all the particular doctrines of the churches are optional (Ecumenism, 24).

The toll on Rahner's expressway to the unity of the church, relegating all the particular doctrines to optional status, is too costly (Ecumenism, 23). The churches treasure their doctrines. They are not human discoveries or inventions, but God's gifts. They are not optional or negotiable. "If faith is, as we believe, a matter of fidelity to the truth given in Jesus Christ, unity must not be purchased at the expense of honest conviction" (Ecumenism, 23). Now this "truth given in Jesus Christ" is embodied in the many traditions— Lutheran, Methodist, Orthodox, Quaker, Episcopalian, Roman Catholic, etc.—of Christianity. How can an authentic unity result from infidelity to these traditions?

The Rahner–Fries proposal would create a "nondescript union of churches…impoverishing to all concerned." Since it would achieve unity by eliminating the particular and distinctive, it must be rejected as "excessively reductionistic" (Ecumenism, 24). It offers only a pseudo-church of the least common denominator. Its members' commitment would be lessened by the extent to which their own particular church's doctrines had been made marginal for membership.

"The world does not need a gigantic supermarket church that stands for nothing in particular, while offering everything to everybody" (Ecumenism, 24). A church created by a consensus on the minimum necessary would be even more vulnerable to our aggressively secularist culture than the particular churches are already. Such a church cannot stand "against the world for the world" (the title of the 1976 Hartford Appeal which Dulles signed and supported), since it would be too much like the world. If the distinctive truths and unique heritages of the churches are whittled away, the united church cannot witness against the culture since it has no distinctive truths and convictions to stand upon.

What the supermarket has done to the grocery business, ecumenism could, if unchecked, do for the churches. A single united church, though it might boast many millions of members, would be bland and unexciting. Constrained to satisfy an enormous and widely diverse constituency, the mass-church would be even less capable of speaking out prophetically than are our presently divided confessions. If the official leadership of such a Christian conglomerate were to take any controversial positions, many of the members would have just cause for resentment. Caught up in this gargantuan organization, they would have no escape from its determinations except by fleeing into the outer darkness of a churchless existence (Strategies, 180).

For Dulles, the divisiveness of particular churches' doctrines must be handled differently. This way is outlined in his final four theses. His seventh thesis states that *"…the churches should insist only on the doctrinal minimum required for a mature and authentic Christian faith, and that doctrines formulated in response to past historical crises should be carefully reviewed to see whether they must be imposed as tests of orthodoxy today"* (Paths, 41). Then the churches can draw closer together when, according to his Thesis 8, *"Through reinterpretation in a broader hermeneutical context, the limitations of controverted doctrinal formulations can often be overcome, so that they gain wider acceptability"* (Paths, 44).

The most exacting reinterpretation may not, however, secure this wider acceptability. Certain doctrinal formulations may still be resisted when they do not seem to convey adequately the riches of one church's heritage. Still, *"In some cases substantive agreement can be reached between two parties without the imposition of identical doctrinal formulations on each"* (Paths, 44) when differing churches realize that their particular doctrinal formulae are complementary. The *Filioque* issue is a classic example (Paths, 44–45).

Unity is still possible even where this kind of substantive agreement cannot be reached. His Thesis 10 states, *"For the sake of doctrinal agreement, the binding formulations of each tradition must be carefully scrutinized and jointly affirmed with whatever modifications, explanations, or reservations are required in order to appease the legitimate misgivings of the partner churches"* (Paths, 46). The Final Report of the first Anglican–Roman Catholic International Commission provides one good example of partner churches working toward this joint affirmation, as does *Papal Primacy and the Universal Church*, the work of the Lutheran–Catholic Dialogue when Dulles was a member.

For Rahner, dialogue over the churches' differing doctrines would continue *after* the reunion had been effected and would help to solidify the unity already achieved. For Dulles, on the other hand, dialogue over the churches' differing doctrines lays the foundation for reunion and the work may not be completed in historical time. In a classic understatement: "considerable time and effort will be needed to achieve the kind of doctrinal agreement needed for full communion between churches as widely separated as the Orthodox, Protestant, Anglican, and Roman Catholic" (Paths, 46). Even if that agreement were reached, only "the doctrinal basis for full communion will have been laid" (Paths, 47). Presumably, the canonical and liturgical (and financial!) bases would remain on the ecumenical agenda.

Though Dulles contends that the goal of ecumenical dialogue can no longer realistically be taken as the full visible unity of the churches, he wants dialogue to continue. It can show the world that mutual respect and understanding are possible, despite deep and persistent disagreements. Dialogue also "increases the communion among Christians and diminishes the scandal arising from their mutual opposition" (Paths, 47). Through dialogue the gifts and graces of each church may enrich the others and each church may come to a less inadequate expression of its own faith (Ecumenism, 24). Still, Dulles does not shrink from Rahner's harsh alternative. He has the courage to argue that unity is not real-

istically achievable because it has to be secured on broader doctrinal grounds than "merely" the scriptures and the creeds.

Unity of the Churches, however, already responds to Dulles'
concerns.

Dulles thinks that "epistemological tolerance" (Unity, 38)
makes each church's particular doctrines optional, resulting in
eucharistic celebrations of a unity that does not actually exist.
Rahner answers,

> ...the unity of faith which actually exists in the Catholic
> church and must be legitimate is different from the unity
> of faith which one silently presupposes in theoretical
> ecclesiology to be self-evident. One considers the latter
> unity to be clear agreement (explicit, or at least implicit)
> to everything taught offically as binding dogma. But the
> unity of faith concretely realized within the Catholic
> church is also differentiated from the theoretically pos-
> tulated unity of faith. And yet it is legitimate, and must
> be explicitly acknowledged as such (39).

The actual practice of the churches shows that the unity of
faith is not secured by members' explicit adherence to every
authoritative teaching of their church. As they share life with the
community of faith, they give proof of their inchoate but real
acceptance of its doctrines. To demand more than this as the price
of unity is to demand more of the other churches than is demanded
within each church.

The partner churches' agreement not to condemn each
other's doctrines nor to impose their own as a condition for unity
does not make their particular doctrines optional. Rahner agrees
with Dulles: these doctrines are a precious legacy given by God to
each church; they cannot be surrendered without infidelity.

So Thesis II "does not mean that...that which the existing
churches have counted as a 'definitive' part of the substance of
their faith, should be changed or relinquished" (25, 112–113). The

united church embodies reconciled diversity. There each partner church can still recognize and treasure God's work in its own particular history (34) and live with other churches in a communion of communions. The particular doctrines are not marginalized in the Rahner proposal. On the contrary, they remain on the agenda for continuing discussion among the partner churches, but they do not divide them.

Rahner might, then, answer Dulles, "You admit that a 'large measure' of doctrinal agreement is substantiated in the common acceptance of the Scriptures and the Creeds. You reject the simplistic identification of unity with uniformity (Catholicity, 80). Doesn't this unity of faith have to be reflected in the life of the churches? Why not intensify the call for visible unity which you made in the context of the Lutheran-Catholic Dialogue? At that point, there was no full agreement, just convergence, on the *iure divino* character of the Papacy. Still, you said, 'But we suggest… that a distinct canonical status may be worked out by which Lutherans could be in official communion with the church of Rome' (Primacy, 38). And I agree with you!"

Rahner and Fries would also claim that Dulles caricatures their proposal. It is not "excessively reductionistic" nor does it lead to "a nondescript union of churches" because they explicitly reject any unity that would eliminate the uniqueness of a partner church. They agree that church life based on a minimal common consensus is an uninhabitable abstraction (112–113). The foundation of the scriptures and the creeds is no minimalistic basis for unity. It is, rather, the maximum by contrast with the world's convictions (Einigung, 164). In these we find what differentiates the churches decisively from a world where atheism and relativism hold sway (Unity, 16). A church founded on the scriptures and creeds will never blend into a culture that denies the existence or relevance of God.

Not only are there answers to Dulles' objections in *Unity of the Churches* but there are important theological agreements between him and Rahner, which make their disagreement all the more surprising. For instance, Dulles recognizes the ecumenical imperative for effective church mission. A divided Christian church is a weakened sacrament.

Elsewhere I have argued that the spectre of secularism as the relentless exclusion of the transcendent from human life led Dulles to misconstrue Rahner's proposal as reductionistic (Nilson, Unity). Dulles fears that a unified church would lack what it needs to oppose our secularist culture. The chief danger is the church's "excessive and indiscreet accommodation" (Uneasy, 59). As churches become less distinct from other movements, they lose members (Ecumenism, 22). Then secularism has even more leeway to remove God from culture and, therefore, hope from the marginalized and powerless (Mission, 22–23).

For Dulles, the churches' mission today demands that they become not more like each other but less like the culture that threatens to subvert them. "The Church [like Jesus] must question the world's questions, and in this way challenge the values and priorities on which those questions are based" (Modernity, 86). But churches can only do this when they immerse themselves in their own distinctive traditions. This immersion can prevent a "growing pluralism of doctrine and practice from destroying the very identity of the Church" (Ecumenism, 22).

The root of the disagreement between Rahner and Dulles is not, therefore, theological or even religious. It is their two quite different assessments of the conditions of contemporary culture and their implications for the church's mission. Dulles' critique, therefore, leaves the philosophical and theological grounding of the Rahner-Fries proposal intact.

Ratzinger's Critique

Joseph Ratzinger's views of the Rahner–Fries proposal are important in virtue of the position he holds, prefect (or chief executive) of the Vatican's Congregation for the Doctrine of the Faith. As such, Ratzinger is the pope's main theological advisor. He also reviews the doctrinal content of all documents and position papers that other Vatican congregations and offices issue. The Pontifical Council for Promoting Christian Unity, for example, "must proceed in close connection with the Congregation for the Doctrine of the Faith, especially when it is a matter of publishing public documents and declarations" (Directory, 6, n. 7).

Initially, Ratzinger made some brief, disparaging remarks about the proposal. Echoing Ols, he accused Rahner and Fries of skipping irresponsibly the question of truth by means of a few moves of ecclesiastical politics (Luther, 114; Einheit, 577). He characterized their proposal as "Ein-Par-force-Ritt zur Einheit... eine Kunstfigur theologischer Akrobatik, die leider der Realität nicht standhalt" (Einheit, 573). Interestingly, the *Communio* translation preserves his image, "an artificial exploit of theological acrobatics" [216], while the translation in *Church, Ecumenism and Politics* protects Ratzinger by omitting the phrase altogether [108]. Fries himself reports Ratzinger to have said "Kunstgriff," instead of Kunstfigur" [Einigung, 160]). When a firestorm of criticism broke out, he felt compelled to explain his reasons for dismissing the work of his former colleagues. It is puzzling that he then presented further caricatures of the Rahner–Fries proposal, which are incongruent with his theological acumen and learning and unworthy of the office he holds.

Like Ols, Ratzinger asserts that a unity of the church exists already, as if to say that the quest for reunion is less urgent than ecumenists seem to think. It is, however, the unity that belongs to the Roman Catholic Church (115, 120, 121–122). Thus he mutes, even if he does not completely ignore, the damage created by continuing divisions. Ratzinger seems immune to the passion behind the words of UR, #1: "Without doubt, this discord openly contradicts the will of Christ, provides a stumbling block [*scandalo*] to the world, and inflicts damage on the most holy cause of proclaiming the good news to every creature."

He joins the consensus of friends and foes alike that Thesis II on epistemological tolerance is the cornerstone of the entire

Rahner–Fries proposal (124). Without epistemological tolerance, their argument that unity is a present possibility falls apart. Once again, here is the thesis:

> Beyond that, a realistic principle of faith should apply: Nothing may be rejected decisively and confessionally in one partner church which is binding dogma in another partner church. Furthermore, beyond [the content specified in] Thesis I no explicit and positive confession in one partner church is imposed as dogma obligatory for another partner church. This is left to a broader consensus in the future. This applies especially to authentic but undefined doctrinal decrees of the Roman church, particularly with regard to ethical questions. According to this principle only that would be done which is already practice in every church today (Unity 7, 25).

Now this situation, according to Ratzinger, means "nobody knowing any longer exactly whether he or she has correctly understood the Church's teaching (based on the bible), whether he or she has rightly grasped the other's theology" (130). It means "the general fog [where] nobody can see the other and no one sees the truth" (131), and "nobody can judge his or her own thinking" (131). He even calls Rahner's description, "intellectual political situation," a "linguistic monstrosity" (130) and concludes that the unity of faith postulated by the Rahner proposal is a sheer "formal unity without any clear content...fundamentally no unity at all..." (131). Its content is a bare minimum that results from "reducing everything to the first two ecumenical councils" (133). All the doctrines beyond that, whether those of the united Church or those of the divided churches, are relegated to epistemological tolerance. The result is an "ecumenism in reverse" (133) that returns to 400 A.D. and then attempts the impossible task of going forward again from that point.

Ratzinger claims that the faith and the good sense of the

Christian people would make them rebel against this ersatz unity. He quotes Rahner's advice for dealing with the Christian people's initial reluctance: "'those responsible for this [Church] leadership...[must] exert themselves with sufficient zeal among members of their Churches to bring about an understanding of this decision [for reunion].'" (128) This, sputters Ratzinger, is "completely intolerable...a misunderstanding which manipulates consciences in an impermissible way and noticeably threatens the internal cohesion of the Catholic Church" (128). Church leadership represents the Spirit-given faith of the whole people of God. It is not an elite that coerces the membership into accepting the unacceptable (129). Church leaders articulate the faith of the church; they do not create it (130).

Now these are obvious and therefore puzzling misrepresentations of Rahner's thinking. First, why would the efforts of church leaders to foster people's understanding of a decision for unity constitute manipulation any more than attempts like *Humanae Vitae* or *Veritatis Splendor* to shape their undestanding? Would they not be a legitimate exercise of the teaching office, just as these encyclicals are? If so, how would this threaten the Catholic Church's cohesion?

Second, Rahner's point is not that "nobody know[s] any longer exactly whether he or she has correctly understood the Church's teaching (based on the bible), whether he or she has rightly grasped the other's theology" (130), but that nobody can be certain that a church-dividing issue truly lurks within the tangled differences of language, philosophy, and cultural presuppositions. Our intellectual wealth creates a new context: "Here... one knows overwhelmingly more than previously—too much to prevent one single theologian, to say nothing of a single Christian, from becoming ever more impotent in comparison to this existing body of theological knowledge" (Unity, 29). Fries is right in pointing out that, "This problem becomes acute for the ecumenical question in so far as the unity of faith cannot be conceived without a certain unity of theology as well" (Thesis II, 12).

We are obliged to theologize as we try to discern the necessary degree of unity of faith but our intellectual wealth compels us to be modest in our expectations of the results.

But not too modest! In other places, Rahner has shown how our new situation calls for the development of "indirect methods" in theology (Methodology, 74–79). This insight is later developed into a theological specialty in its own right, whose first articulation is *Foundations of Christian Faith* (7–10).

Epistemological tolerance is, therefore, not a Rahnerian term for general and irreducible ignorance, an excuse for avoiding the hard work of thought, an empty lot where a counterfeit unified church can be constructed. Epistemological tolerance is, instead, a way to deal with the unmasterable quantity and complexity of scholarship today and the consequent unattainability of certitude in theology. If a certainly correct and comprehensive understanding of the church's teachings and of a classical theologian's work were relatively easy to reach, it is hard to understand why theological libraries are full, new theological periodicals are founded to complement older ones, and those who specialize in just one book of the Bible or one classical theologian may not be able to keep abreast of the discussion in their field. Consider too that Rahner's description predates that intellectual cornucopia, the Internet!

Rahner's point is that church unity is impossible if it requires us to be certain of the ultimate complementarity of all the docrines of the partner churches. That will not and cannot happen, especially as Christians from the third world's cultural horizons enter the ecumenical conversation. If we cannot be certain before God that our fidelity to the gospel requires our continuing divisions, by what right do we continue them?

If Rahner is mistaken on this point, he has good company. For instance, Ratzinger himself realizes that "…the question of the mutual relationship between the 'I' and the 'we', between the evidence provided by the individual conscience and the joint evidence of the one faith which we can only receive by sharing in believing, has for too long not been satisfactorily explained"

(130). Indeed, this is one way of describing the situation which dictates epistemological tolerance.

Walter Kasper has maintained that the Catholic tradition actually demands less than Fries and Rahner have proposed: "As part of a long tradition of interpreting Hebrews 11:6, one can therefore say that whoever believes that God exists and that he is the salvation of humanity believes not only a part but implicitly the whole faith. That one is in invisible fellowship with the universal church, which extends well beyond its institutional boundaries" (27).

Fries appeals to the 1975 Roman Catholic synod of all the dioceses in the then Federal Republic of Germany, including all the West German bishops:

> A unification in faith is not possible as long as one church sees itself compelled to reject a binding doctrine of another church as contrary to revelation. On the other hand, the Catholic church does not require of its members that they affirm in the same manner all expressions and derivations that have occurred in the history of the faith as taught and lived. Even less does she expect this of other Christians. A wide scope for ecumenical possibilities is opened here, which is to be probed in discussion with the churches (Thesis II, 9).

Rahner does not want to drag us back to 400 A.D. nor does he call for shunting doctrinal differences aside. He simply sees all that is required for a unity of faith expressed in the scriptures and creeds. We can join together now. Reunion does not make our differences negligible; rather, it changes their significance. Instead of justifying our divisions, they help to solidify our unity.

Still, Ratzinger has no sympathy for Rahner–Fries' Thesis I. It appears to him a minimal or even empty basis for unity (133). Yet the scriptures and creeds seem minimal so long as one thinks only in the context of Christianity. Placed in contrast to widespread western secularism and the great non-Christian religions like Hinduism and Islam, the scriptures and creeds constitute a remarkable maximum.

Ratzinger misses the importance of Thesis I because the importance of the "hierarchy of truths" in UR, #11 is lost on him. Certainly, all the truths of faith are important; none may be surrendered or lost in the one church to be. Yet not every doctrine of every church needs to be accepted by every other partner church. Doctrines are related differently to the core and foundation of the Christian faith, Jesus Christ.

As Fries points out, Ratzinger himself has utilized the same principle in arguing that "Unification could occur on the basis, on the one hand, that the east renounce opposing the western development of the second millennium as heretical, and accept the Catholic church in the form which it has arrived at in this development as orthodox and legitimate; while on the other hand, the church in the west recognizes the orthodoxy and legitimacy of the church of the east in the form which it has maintained" (Thesis II, 10).

Ratzinger's distortions of the Rahner–Fries proposal are disturbing. Anyone who has studied their book carefully and knows Rahner's work cannot characterize it as Ratzinger does. The chasm between his talents and accomplishments and his shoddy analysis of their work is so wide as to be incredible.

Roman Catholic Support for Rahner–Fries

The positions held by Ols and Ratzinger (the former unofficial and the latter official) are significant, but not their critiques of the Rahner–Fries proposal because they misconstrue it. Two other Roman Catholic voices deserve attention here. Both are familiar with the proposal. True, neither one openly endorses it, yet it is telling that neither criticizes it and both provide additional theological support for it.

Walter Kasper wrote "Basic Consensus and Church Fellowship" for a conference held in early 1987 while he was still a professor at Tübingen. The respect he commanded in Rome had been signaled earlier by his appointment as secretary to the Extraordinary Synod of Bishops (November–December 1985), which was summoned to celebrate and appropriate Vatican II. Later, he was ordained bishop of Rottenburg-Stuttgart. This is not the career path of some "theological acrobat" who would subvert the Catholic faith to secure church unity.

In his essay, Kasper notes that the churches are not divided because they differ in the fundamental truths of Christian faith but because they differ in other relatively marginal ways, e.g. liturgy, polity. When these ways are probed more deeply, they reveal themselves to be simply reflections of different theologies, not manifestations of church–dividing differences. "Theological systems are church divisive only as long as they interpret and systematize creedal issues divisively. If that is not the case, they represent legitimate differences between theological schools within a larger unity. Then one should speak of a basic problem in theology rather than basic disagreement" (23). The basic differences or disagreements that alone can justify the churches' continuing separation remain elusive.

Kasper points out that the bi-lateral and multi-lateral dialogues have discerned fundamental unity and sought fundamental difference. Yet the fundamental difference in faith has not been identified and expressed. All the churches stand firmly and nonnegotiably on the creeds as the "least inadequate" articulations of the fundamentals of the faith they hold. Indeed, important issues remain and crucial questions remain unanswered, but they are issues and questions within the parameters of a fundamental unity of faith.

In the same essay, Kasper even defines the scope of the unity of faith required for the unity of the churches more narrowly than Rahner and Fries do. He draws on the scholastic notion of "implicit faith," whereby the fundamental truths of faith include all the other truths objectively and not simply by virtue of the good intention of the inculpably ignorant believer. He appeals to Aquinas to support his claim that "basic consensus already implies full consensus in the whole truth" (27).

And what are the fundamental truths that include all the others objectively? "As part of a long tradition of interpreting Hebrews 11:6, one can...say that whoever believes that God exists and that he is the salvation of humanity believes not only a part but implicitly the whole faith" (27).

Now "implicit faith" is characteristic of individuals, not churches. Nonetheless, it is "helpful as long as it does not need to require of the other partner explicit acceptance of all distinctive doctrines beyond the basic consensus (for instance, the more recent mariological dogmas). It is sufficient if the ecumenical partner acknowledges such developments to be basically legitimate on the basis of the gospel and if they are no longer condemned as contrary to the gospel. Where this happens, it does not mean that criticism is suspended, but that there is an intentional assent to the whole truth" (28). In effect, Kasper is saying, "I agree with Rahner on Thesis I and II—and I would even be willing to be more tolerant on Thesis I."

Paralleling the Rahner–Fries proposal, he marks out areas of discussion that would remain on the agenda for discussion of the partner churches subsequent to their reunion. Diversity is possible and necessary in understanding the church as mediator of salvation (38–39) and in understanding the relation of the teaching office to the Scriptures (34). Yet Kasper is well aware of the difficulties entailed in this further work: "such unity in diversity also represents quite an imposition and is impossible without heartfelt conversion" (28). Nonetheless, the churches' fundamental agreement in faith and their new shared life enhance the probability that their differences will turn out to be complementary, even though they be as crucial as the structure of the act of faith (which Ratzinger sees as one wall standing between Lutherans and Catholics; 109–114).

Pierre Duprey was a priest on the staff of the Vatican's Secretariat for Promoting Christian Unity when he contributed a paper to the same 1987 conference. Previously, he had served as a Vatican delegate to ARCIC-I that produced the ground-breaking *Final Report*. Subsequently, he was ordained a bishop and appointed under-secretary, or second in command, to Cardinal Edward Cassidy at the Secretariat. Like Kasper's, this is not the biographical sketch of a Roman Catholic "theological acrobat."

Duprey does not allude to the Rahner proposal even in a footnote, as Kasper does, but he provides cogent support for it.

The structuring principle of the "hierarchy of truths" (UR, #11) is Jesus Christ himself. In accepting Christ as savior, we embrace the entirety of revelation, the total mystery of salvation (140). The other truths of the "hierarchy" are, therefore, not logical explications of a comprehensive core axiom that unfold into a Euclidean interlacing of doctrinal propositions. Instead, they are explanations and protections of the integrity of the central mystery of Jesus Christ as savior (140). To grasp how and why they are ordered as they are, we must live them ever more deeply, allowing them to draw us more deeply into relationship with Christ.

Duprey also notes that, while Roman Catholicism affirms seven sacraments, it maintains a hierarchy of importance within them. For Aquinas (and for the Constitution on the Liturgy of Vatican II, which devotes a whole chapter to it), the eucharist is core, central, and primary (140). Thus Duprey shows how the Roman Catholic Church could join with a partner church that accepted only baptism and eucharist, provided that this partner church did not reject the remaining five sacraments as contrary to the gospel and was willing to discuss them with its new Roman Catholic partner.

Finally, Duprey gives an example of what Rahner and Fries mean by refusing to demand more of our partner churches than we do of ourselves. He recalls an encounter with a representative of the United Church of Christ from Zaire, who told him, "You Catholics are a collection of confessional families. You place alongside an episcopal structure the powerful presbyteral structures of your religious orders, each of which has its own way of accentuating and organizing its conception of the Christian life. You keep all that in unity, even though not always without tensions, because you all acknowledge the authority and magisterium of discernment found in the bishop of Rome" (145). Duprey underlines the moral of the story: "The diversities which our Zairean friend pointed to were maintained in unity because they were located in the life of the church, which they enriched by their very diversity. Only the church can maintain in unity the various attempts, always approximate, to express and live the hierarchy of truths. That hierarchy will never be disclosed to us..." until the eschaton (145).

Like Kasper, Duprey could easily have used the 1987 Puerto Rico meeting to criticize the Rahner–Fries proposal. After all, this conference on "Fundamental Consensus and Church Fellowship" could hardly ignore the most prominent and debated Roman Catholic proposal for unity founded on a basic consensus, *Unity of the Churches*. But Duprey does not attack it. Instead he points to one reason why the Roman Catholic Church may still be ecumenically immobile:

> ...the very progress of partial agreements frightens people, so that they take refuge in looking for fundamental differences, which will not be the root from which fundamental healing comes but rather an excuse for telling ourselves that such healing is impossible. I can only reject with all the force of my Christian conviction this form of defeatism.
>
> The progress of partial agreements provokes the desire for a global agreement or (why not admit it) the fear of such an agreement, a fear which is connected with that question of identity fashionable today when so many personalities do not reach maturity. In fact, I believe immaturity is the reason for the fashion, since problems of identity are typically problems of adolescence, and adolescence is not just a question of age (143).

Like Kasper, Duprey is saying, "I agree with Rahner."

If the arguments of this chapter are sound, *Unity of the Churches. An Actual Possibility* is no book like *Secular City* or *Honest to God*, a period piece that provokes interest and excitement among theologians and non-theologians, and even an article in *Time*, but then looks dated and even quaint after a few years. The Rahner–Fries book constitutes an agenda and a serious obligation for the leaders of the churches, especially the Roman Catholic Church. The unity of faith required for the unity of the churches now already exists. Once we recognize it, we cannot scurry around in search of reasons to justify our continuing isolation from one another—because there are none. The only course is to make the changes, formulate the policies, and establish the structures that will render our unity in Jesus Christ visible and operative.

Can the Roman Catholic Church approach the other Christian churches and communities as truly equal partners in a common quest for unity? If the Roman Church holds that the church of Christ subsists in her (LG, #8), that it is "through Christ's Catholic Church alone, which is the all-embracing means of salvation, that the fullness of the means of salvation can be obtained" (UR, #3), and that a church or community not in communion with the pope as the successor of Peter is *ipso facto* "wounded" (CDF, 6/92), must it not be faithful to its identity as such? Is it not reluctantly but clearly obliged to claim a dominance and superiority over the other Christian churches that will obviously be unacceptable to them? In short, can the Roman Catholic Church truly be a "partner church"? This is the issue of the next chapter.

The Roman Church need not wait until it finds enthusiastic collaborators in the struggle toward unity. It can do much to turn suspicious fellow Christians into eager allies by making the changes that demonstrate the sincerity of its ecumenical commitments. The church's official documents have repeatedly underlined the indispensability and centrality of conversion and reform to church unity. Specifically, what do these mean? In particular, what could and should the Roman Church do now to prove to its fellow Christians that it truly seeks unity with them and is ready to suffer what is necessary to secure it? These are the questions of the last chapter.

Chapter Three

THE CHURCHES ARE ACTUALIZATIONS OF CHRISTIANITY

The Roman Catholic Church came later than other churches to the ecumenical table. Its negative judgment of those other churches was fixed at the time of the reformation and remained largely unaltered until Vatican II.

In its interpretation of those four hundred and fifty years, other churches had broken away from the fullness of truth and of the means of salvation given by God in the church of Jesus Christ, the Roman Catholic Church. At best, these groups were simply truncated and distorted versions of Christianity. At worst, they were the historical residue of ignorant, unjustified, and sinful rebellions against the divinely established authority of the Roman Church.

These counterfeits were not even genuine churches at all. They commanded the loyalty of millions only because those millions through no fault of their own were ignorant of the facts. If they were unfortunate enough to be born and raised in a non-Catholic community, however, they could still be saved. Their ignorance of which church was truly the church of Jesus Christ might not be blameworthy. It could be presumed that they would become Roman Catholics when they discovered their error. To Catholics' joy and sometimes smug satisfaction, other Christians did now and then join the Roman Catholic Church.

In this interpretation of the reformation, the unity of Christianity would be restored only when the counterfeit churches returned to the "Roman obedience." Then the western religious landscape would be littered with ecclesial suicides, since this return would require each church to give up its distinctive identity and gifts. The ecumenism of return—officially set forth in

52

Mortalium Animos of Pius XI in 1928 and briefly revived in Daniel Ols' critique of Rahner and Fries—was buttressed ideologically by the neo-scholasticism that had dominated Roman Catholic theology and Vatican policy from the election of Leo XIII in 1878 to the dawn of Vatican II (Nilson, Aquinas, 23–29).

In the neo-scholastic mentality (which Bernard Lonergan has described and diagnosed as the "classicist world-view"), historical development has no bearing on the substance of truth. Reality is constituted by a systematically ordered hierarchy of timeless essences, differentiated by their accidental features. To know the essence is to know the truth of the thing. So

> ...one can apprehend man abstractly through a defini-
> tion that applies *omni et soli* and through properties
> verifiable in every man. In this fashion one knows man
> as such; and man as such, precisely because he is an
> abstraction, also is unchanging. It follows...that on this
> view one is never going to arrive at any exigence for
> changing forms, structures, methods, for all change
> occurs in the concrete, and on this view the concrete is
> always omitted (Classicist, 5).

History will not, therefore, display change and development to the classicist mind but a variety of accidental features, which modify but do not alter the substance. The power of particularities, such as individual personality traits, social class, educational attainment, ethnic heritage, national experience, to open certain perspectives on reality and to close off others is barely surmised, much less accounted for, in the classicist world-view.

It is ironic that Pius X's anti-modernist crusade and its aftermath promoted the collapse of the neo-scholastic hegemony in the church. In his encyclical *Pascendi Dominici Gregis* (1907), Pius ordered that those who showed a love of new ideas were not to be ordained to the priesthood. If such novelty lovers were teachers, they had to be deprived of their positions. Creative and constructive philosophy and theology became dangerous. To admit that one read Kant and Hegel was to become a marked man. So Catholic scholars migrated to the safer territory of history to escape suspicion and harassment. They devoted their time to research and writing on the medieval period and its great thinkers, especially Aquinas whose accomplishments, according to Leo XIII, made the others superfluous because "His teaching is so formed and buttressed by principles with such breadth of application that it meets the needs not only of a single age but those of all times and it is very capable of conquering the errors which constantly arise" (Aubert, 160; translation mine).

Scholars who may have expected to find uniformity and continuity in Roman Catholic history and thought found variety and and change, instead. They discovered that Aquinas and the other giants of the past (e.g. Augustine, Bonaventure, Duns Scotus) were not automatons cranking out applications of the timelessly true philosophy (the so-called *philosophia perennis*) to questions as they arose. Nor did they simply generate logical deductions from that philosophy, like geometric proofs from a few faith axioms. Rather, Augustine, Aquinas, Bonaventure, Bernard and the rest were gifted people of faith who struggled to understand faith's meaning in and for their own age. Their thinking reflected accurately and preeminently their times. Research showed how they developed their ideas and even changed their positions.

The research that undergirded the Roman Catholic liturgical revival was also turning up evidence of a diverse church changing throughout the centuries. In adapting itself, the church had not surrendered to the corrosive powers of anti-Christian culture. Rather, it had proven its Spirit-given vitality and the inexhaustibility of the good news it proclaimed, whose body it was, Jesus Christ, God with us. Gradually, historical scholarship made it impossible to say that "The church never changes." The touchstone formulated by Vincent of Lerins for the faith of the church as held "ubique, semper, ab omnibus" was getting harder and harder to maintain without considerable nuance.

What the Roman Catholic Church learned from these studies is distilled in Vatican II's *Gaudium et Spes*, the Pastoral Constitution on the Church in the Modern World. The passage has to be quoted in full:

> Just as it is in the world's interest to acknowledge the Church as an historical reality, and to recognize her good influence, so the Church knows how richly she has profited by the history and development of humanity. Thanks to the experience of past ages, the progress of the sciences, and the treasures hidden in the various forms of human culture, human nature itself is more clearly revealed and new roads to truth are opened. These benefits profit the Church, too. For, from the beginning of her history, she has learned to express the message of Christ with the help of the ideas and terminology of various peoples, and has tried to clarify it with the wisdom of philosophers, too.
>
> Her purpose has been to adapt the gospel to the grasp of all as well as to the needs of the learned, insofar as such was appropriate. Indeed, this accommodated preaching of the revealed Word ought to remain the law of all evangelization. For thus each nation develops the ability to express Christ's message in its own way. At the same time, a vital exchange is fostered between the Church and the diverse cultures of people....With the help of the Holy Spirit, it is the task of the entire People of God, especially pastors and theologians, to hear, distinguish, and interpret the many voices of our age, and to judge them in the light of the divine Word. In this way, revealed truth can always be more deeply penetrated, better understood, and more aptly set forth (GS, #44; see also LG, #13).

Insights like these helped to lay "the ecumenism of return" to rest. Vatican II initiated a new Roman Catholic understanding and appreciation of the other Christian churches. As UR, #3 admits, the Roman Catholic Church bears its share of responsibility for the divisions. Many people could not recognize the true Church of Jesus Christ in the Church of Rome. So they left it in order to be faithful to Christ. Those now "born into these communities and …instilled therein with Christ's faith" (UR, #3) remain in that church "which each regards as his Church *and, indeed, God's*" (UR, #1; emphasis added). It is simplistic as well as insulting to maintain that sinfulness and stupidity sufficiently explain the foundation and perdurance of those churches.

Still, the Roman Catholic Church does not consider itself a Christian church like the others in every fundamental respect. It claims that the Church of Jesus Christ *subsists* in it and it alone.

> This Church, constituted and organized in the world as a society, subsists in the Catholic Church, which is governed by the successor of Peter and by the bishops in union with that successor, although many elements of sanctification and of truth can be found outside of her visible structure. These elements, however, as gifts properly belonging to the church of Christ, possess an inner dynamism toward Catholic unity (LG, #8).

This text signaled a signficant change in the official Roman Catholic self-understanding. Here the council refused to endorse the teaching of Pius XII in *Mystici Corporis Christi* (1943) that the true church of Christ and the Roman Catholic Church were one and the same. So this text expressed the theological grounding for the church's belated but enthusiastic embrace of the ecumenical movement. It acknowledges other Christians as true brothers and sisters and acknowledges other churches as also part of the one church of Christ.

The Roman Catholic Church's self-understanding that the

church of Christ *subsists* or continues in it is repeated in the new
Ecumenical Directory (#17). In the Decree on Ecumenism, the
implications of this view are made explicit:

> ...it is through Christ's Catholic Church alone, which
> is the all-embracing means of salvation, that the full-
> ness of the means of salvation can be obtained. It was to
> the apostolic college alone, of which Peter is the head,
> that we believe our Lord entrusted all the blessings of
> the New Covenant, in order to establish on earth the
> one Body of Christ into which all those should be fully
> incorporated who already belong in any way to God's
> People (UR, #3).

The fullness of the means of salvation with which Christ endowed
his church is available, therefore, in the Roman Catholic Church
alone.

In no way, however, does this self-understanding negate the
legitimacy of the other churches. It does not deny their authenticity
as Christian. Vatican II does not warrant a new version of the ecumenism of return, whereby non-Catholics who *ipso facto* dwell in
the partial must now come to the fullness found only in Roman
Catholicism.

Other significant statements of the council suggest a form of
parity between the Roman Catholic Church and the other Christian
churches. For instance, the church's reality is not clear to outsiders
who see lack of fervor and commitment in it (UR, # 4). The sinfulness of its members obscures its identity as the true Church
of Jesus Christ. "For although the Catholic Church has been
endowed with all divinely revealed truth and with all means of
grace, her members fail to live by them with all the fervor they
should. As a result, the radiance of the Church's face shines less
brightly in the eyes of our separated brethren and of the world at
large, and the growth of God's kingdom is retarded" (UR, #4).

So the Roman Church can look like massive, corporate infidelity to the gospel. Today many Christians actually do turn their backs on it because the church denies non-ordained people a significant role in its decision-making, deprives many of its members of the eucharist in order to maintain the tradition of priestly celibacy, and excludes women from serving as bishops, priests, and deacons for reasons that are unconvincing even to many of its own members. Non-Catholics do not see how policies like these reflect or advance the good news that Christ is and brings.

To these people, their own churches seem to be more authentic reflections of what Christ means, asks, and promises, a more credible claim to be the church of Jesus Christ. People join a particular church and remain in it because they see it as the least inadequate corporate interpretation and response to the meaning of Jesus Christ. To them, their church is the most reliable guide and support for ever greater immersion into the Christian mystery (UR, #1).

If the church of Christ subsists in the Roman Catholic Church but is not identical with it, Catholics must respect and reverence "the riches of Christ" in fellow Christians. The council calls them to remember that what the Holy Spirit accomplishes in separated brothers and sisters can contribute to our own growth and deepening as Christians and even be "a more ample realization of the very mystery of Christ and the Church" (UR, #4).

The members of these churches, therefore, rightly consider their churches as their religious home; the settings where they first heard and began to live the gospel, where they are formed in discipleship, where they experience "the riches of Christ" and experience their church as God's (UR, #1). They cannot simply leave their churches nor allow their distinctive Christian traditions to evaporate in a homogenized church of the future. Their loyalty is born of and borne by grace. Thus, Pope Paul VI was both wise and reassuring when he promised that there would be no lessening of the worthy patrimony of the Anglican Communion when at last she and the Roman Catholic Church embraced in the one true Church of Christ (Remarks, 5).

A third significant statement from UR admits that the Roman

Church itself is hurt by the continuing divisions: "the Church...
finds it more difficult to express in actual life her full catholicity in
all its aspects" (#4). In the May 1992 letter from the CDF to the
Catholic bishops on the church as communion, the point was reaffirmed. Churches out of communion with Rome are "wounded"
since the ministry of the bishop of Rome is integral to each local
church. Yet the Roman church sustains a wound by being separated
from its brothers and sisters, a point obscured by the faulty translation discussed in Chapter One.

People do not see the full scope of Catholic fullness that subsists in the Roman Church because Christian divisions hide it.
Insofar as this church is self-satisfied and diffidently committed to
ecumenism, there is no choice for many but to remain in those
churches which most enable them to live as Christ's disciples.

UR, #12 urges increasing cooperation between Christians so
that the "riches of Christ" given in all the churches of the one
church of Jesus Christ will become our own experience. Then the
necessary and ongoing reform of the church will be intensified.
But Roman Catholicism's defects will be fuzzy or abstract or even
non-existent to Catholics who have little familiarity with the lived
Christianity of their separated sisters and brothers.

The neo-scholastic mentality, with its sense of human nature
as always and everywhere the same, assumed that the Roman
Church could be sufficiently familiar with every culture. All by
itself it could successfully proclaim the gospel everywhere. It saw
no difficulties in the fact that throughout its history, the church's
human face has been largely white, male, and European.

The post-conciliar church knows that the gospel is never proclaimed by culture-free preachers to empty minds. The gospel is
the divinely revealed interpretation of life that encounters those
interpretations of life already embedded in the life-world of the
hearers. A culture is a set of interpretations of the data of individual and social life. It is a vision of what is worth living for and
worth dying for. It delineates both ultimate and proximate values,
as John S. Dunne's work has shown. The gospel thus proposes

truths and values to people who already know truths, live by values, and speak a certain language. So the gospel message has to be translated into the horizons and language of the listeners. As GS, #44 quoted above affirms, effective proclamation and catechesis require painstaking dialogue between those who proclaim the gospel and their hearers.

While the church of Christ subsists in the Roman Catholic Church, this subsistence does not guarantee that in every place and time its evangelization will be successful. The church does not claim that always and everywhere it appropriates the fullness of revealed truth, expresses it adequately, or utilizes the means of salvation perfectly. In the United States, for example, with its fondness for democratic values, Catholicism was and is often taken as a monarchical system. Many citizens are therefore drawn to more participatory forms of Christian life than the Roman Church offers.

Moreover, no one person, group, class, culture or generation can plumb the depths or exhaust the possibilities of the church's endowments. There is an "inescapably valid principle that nobody, in his particular (individual and collective) reality, can realize, all together and at once, everything that Christian grace and revelation has potentially given to both world and history" (Rahner, Unity, 48). Consider the decades it took for the Roman Church to understand this century's ecumenical movement as the Holy Spirit's gift and to enter into it. This church too bears the human burdens of ignorance and cultural relativity.

In Vatican II's injunction that "accommodated preaching of the revealed Word ought to remain the law of all evangelization" (GS, #44) it is easy to overlook the fact that the word of God has been accommodated already. The most successful and enduring instances of accommodated preaching have been institutionalized and they even have names, such as the Evangelical Lutheran Church of America, Methodism, Orthodox, the Southern Baptist Convention, and the Anglican Communion.

Since God wills the salvation of all, the saving grace of Christ is always and everywhere offered to all. There is no evidence or promise that this grace is mediated always and everywhere through the Roman Catholic Church. Millions keep hearing the gospel and following Christ in some church or Christian community other than a church in communion with the bishop of Rome. So "...there is reason to believe that the division of Christians into the major families of theological tradition—denominations—is not in itself scandalous. On the contrary, it can be seen as a necessary condition of the fullest understanding of an infinite and inexhaustible gospel which defies containment within any single form of life and expression" (Ditmanson, 17).

Consequently, the Roman Church can and does understand these churches and communities as nothing less than Spirit-guided interpretations of the gospel (UR, #3), mediating the "riches of Christ" (UR, #4) to and for the cultures composing the human community. Taken together, they are the church of Jesus Christ, the constellation of humanity's answers to the question asked by those who accept the gospel: "Brothers [and sisters], what are we to do?" (Acts 2:37).

Roman Catholicism's seven sacraments are the acts of Christ himself. He unfailingly offers his grace whenever the sacraments are celebrated. Yet the rituals of separated Christians are also "sacred actions of the Christian religion...[which] can truly engender a life of grace, and...[are] capable of providing access to the communion of salvation" (UR, #3). Thus, the qualitative difference between the effects of the seven sacraments and of these other sacred actions in the lives of Christians, Roman Catholic or not, cannot be identified in an a *priori* way; "these separated Churches and Communities...have by no means been deprived of signficance and *importance* in the mystery of salvation" (UR, #3; emphasis added). Consequently, "There is no question of denying that a non-Catholic community, perhaps lacking much in the order of sacrament, can achieve the *res*, the communion of the life of Christ in faith, hope and love more perfectly than many a Catholic community" (Sullivan, 120).

While Vatican II maintains that "...it is through Christ's

Catholic Church alone, which is the all-embracing means of salvation, that the fullness of the means of salvation can be obtained," UR lists "some, even very many, of the most significant elements or endowments which together go to build up and give life to the Church herself... [that] exist outside the visible boundaries of the Catholic Church: the written word of God; the life of grace; faith, hope, and charity, along with other interior gifts of the Holy Spirit and visible elements" (#3). This listing represents a considerable common treasure and a firm foundation for the real but imperfect communion among Christian churches.

This communion is not grounded essentially and primarily in agreed statements or even in shared means of salvation, but in the Christ, whom we all accept and seek to serve. In following Christ, Christians implicitly accept all that Christ gives as means for salvation, even though they may not recognize some of those means as his.

Primacy is the chief example. Roman Catholics hold that papal primacy is essential to the constitution which Christ gives the church. Undeniably, however, primacy is often exercised in a way that obscures its character as Christ's gift. Even so, non-Roman Christians—and Anglicans in an official way—have stated their willingness to accept primacy, if and when it is reformed along more truly gospel lines (*Final Report*, 77–78).

Since the Christian churches are necessary inculturations or interpretations of Christianity, maintaining legitimate diversity in the partner churches, as in the Rahner–Fries proposal (45), is not just a tolerable concession but a serious obligation: "in order to restore communion and unity or preserve them, one must 'impose no burden beyond what is indispensable'" (UR, #18). This legitimate diversity applies even in the realm of doctrine, as Rahner argues in Thesis II.

Thesis II becomes even more cogent in the light of the Christian churches' identities as necessary, distinctive, and corporate interpretations of the meaning of Jesus Christ. The particular doctrines of each church, whether they be formally declared by some form of magisterium or not, are particular answers to critical questions or corrections of certain errors about the meaning of Jesus Christ (CDF, Declaration, 110).

The Christian churches have all had to grapple with questions and oppose errors. Their doctrines are their authoritative responses, cast in language deemed most effective for the historical circumstances. As historical circumstances change, later generations do not surrender or mitigate or explain away the doctrines developed with God's help. Instead, they struggle to understand them and translate them into the idioms of their own age.

The doctrines of one church are responses to challenges that another church may not have faced. Our doctrines may be answers to questions that our fellow Christians had no need to ask. All that is required for unity is that they condemn neither our forebears in faith for having come to these responses nor us for trying to live by them. All we ask is that they be open to understanding why we continue to hold them. To demand that other Christians embrace our doctrines as their own is to impose burdens beyond the necessary.

In 1966 Archbishop Ramsey and Pope Paul VI realized that the quest for unity could not succeed by a method that rehashed historical controversies and stirred the embers of old angers. Thus, they wisely directed the first Anglican–Roman Catholic International Commission to engage in dialogue "founded on the Gospels and the ancient common traditions," a basis that Paul VI himself insisted upon (Hebblethwaite, Paul, 465). They declared their resolve "to promote responsible contacts between their communions in all those spheres of Church life where collaboration is likely to lead to a greater understanding and a deeper charity" (Joint Statement, 669).

The method of ARCIC-I was summarized and approved by John Paul II when he spoke to commission members in 1980: "Your method has been to go behind the habit of thought and expression born and nourished in enmity and controversy, to scrutinize together the great common treasure, to clothe it in language at once traditional and expressive of an age which no longer glories in strife but seeks to come together in listening to the quiet voice of the Spirit" (Welcome, 341).

These statements spring from a partnership that both communions sought to deepen. Bypassing the language born of controversy and immersing themselves anew in the gospels and the common traditions would yield a new appreciation of the treasure we hold in common. It would lead to further collaborative efforts which, in turn, would be the means for God's grace to bring the day of full unity closer.

Many of the hopes that these commitments produced have been squelched. The Anglican–Roman Catholic relationship in particular has been cooled by the Vatican's reactions to priestly and episcopal ordinations of women and by its response to the ARCIC *Final Report*. For instance, "Anglicans cannot pretend to be anything other than disappointed by the Vatican response to ARCIC-I....Hopes for organic unity seem to have faded... Dreams and visions seem to have faded into a mist of disappointment and a mood of resigned realism," said the archbishop of Canterbury ("No pacts," 255).

Yet there is much that Rome can do now to rekindle those hopes for unity in the foreseeable future.

Chapter Four

WHAT THE ROMAN CATHOLIC CHURCH CAN AND MUST DO NOW FOR CHURCH UNITY

> Christ summons the Church, as she goes her pilgrim way, to that continual reformation of which she always has need, insofar as she is an institution of men here on earth. Therefore, if the influence of events or of the times has led to deficiencies in conduct, in Church discipline, or even in the formulation of doctrine (which must be carefully distinguished from the deposit itself of faith), these should be appropriately rectified at the proper moment (UR, #6).

This is the proper moment. Now is the time for reformation and rectification.

During the centuries of isolation from one another, the churches and communions, including the Roman Catholic Church, have developed practices and mentalities that are no longer required for faithful discipleship and effective mission. These may be cherished and habitual. Still, they can be surrendered without infidelity to Christ. Indeed, they may have to be surrendered for the sake of fidelity to Christ. They may be the price that each particular church must pay for the unity that is now critical to the vitality of the whole church of Christ today.

The contemporary ecumenical agenda for the churches is set by the answers to three questions.

The Christian churches should ask themselves, "is there anything in us that we can abandon for the sake of unity?... is there something we can do in order to make us more acceptable to our separated brothers and sisters?" (Orsy, 7/111).

The Christian churches should also ask each other, "What are you ready to surrender and suffer now for sake of unity?"

Other Christians should press the Roman Catholic Church with the question, "What are you ready to surrender and suffer now for the unity which you claim to be eager for?"

Historical scholarship shows how sinfulness and ignorance have divided Christians from one another—and kept them divided. Sinfulness and ignorance affect Roman Catholicism even today and block the path to church unity. So, this church at every level of its communal life needs to make specific, concrete, and actual "that continual reformation of which she always has need" (UR, #6).

This chapter is intended as a contribution to that work.

The "Hierarchy of Truths"

As discussed above, the bishops of the Protestant Episcopal Church in the United States took a radical and prophetic step toward reunion of the churches in 1886. They declared that in matters of church-ordering that were human in origin, their church was ready to sacrifice its own preferences for the sake of unity. They also declared that reunion should not occur by absorption but by ingathering based on the essentials of a common and traditional faith and order.

They held the essentials to be four: the scriptures, the Nicene Creed ("as the sufficient statement of the Christian faith"), the two sacraments of baptism and the supper of the Lord, and the "historic episcopate."

Should any other Christian church be willing to seek reunion on these bases, the bishops declared that they were ready to explore with them how "so priceless a blessing" could come about.

Two years later, the bishops of the worldwide Anglican Communion, assembled at Lambeth, adapted and adopted the Chicago document. The Apostles' Creed was added to the second point and a few other refinements were made. The resulting text has become known as the Chicago–Lambeth Quadrilateral and reaffirmed by every Lambeth Conference since 1888. It is, as J. Robert Wright says, both heritage and vision (44–45).

Seventy-six years later, the bishops of the Roman Catholic Church took a similiar (but certainly not as extensive) step in Vatican II's Decree on Ecumenism.

> Catholic theologians engaged in ecumenical dialogue, while standing fast by the teaching of the Church and searching together with separated brethren into the divine mysteries, should act with love for truth, with charity, and with humility. *When comparing doctrines, they should remember that in Catholic teaching there exists an order or "hierarchy" of truths, since they vary in their relationship to the foundation of the Christian faith.* Thus the way will be opened for this kind of fraternal rivalry to incite all to a deeper realization and a clearer expression of the unfathomable riches of Christ (#11; emphasis added).

Archbishop Andreas Pangrazio, who was apparently the source for the concept of the "hierarchy of truths" in the decree, meant to underline the fact that Christians now already agree on the fundamentals of the faith (Rahner, Hierarchy, 163). Cardinal Frans König later suggested the precise phrase, "hierarchy of truths." The decree establishes the possibility for a reunion of the churches without Roman Catholic insistence that the partner churches accept the doctrines that it defined during the centuries of separation (i.e. the Marian doctrines of the immaculate conception and the assumption, the papal doctrines of primacy and infallibility). Without this official acknowledgment of a hierarchy of truths, Roman Catholic ecumenical efforts would have been throttled from the beginning.

This acknowledgment is helpful and necessary but far from sufficient. The decree does not specify "the foundation of the

Christian faith" nor does it explain why the Roman Catholic Church will be ecumenically crippled until it does specify it. There may be a clue to the content of the foundation of the faith in #12 of the decree that follows next: "Before the whole world, let all Christians profess their faith in God, one and three, in the incarnate Son of God, our Redeemer and Lord." Still, the affirmation of a hierarchy of truths in Catholic teaching, coupled with the lack of clarity in its content, calls the church to an indispensable ecumenical task.

An initial ecumenical effort to clarify the notion has been published as the Sixth Report of the Joint Working Group Between the Roman Catholic Church and the WCC. Further work on the "foundation of Christian faith" and the hierarchy of truths is still needed for the Roman Catholic Church to fulfill its own ecumenical mandate: "...this sacred synod confirms what previous councils and Roman pontiffs have proclaimed: in order to restore communion and unity or preserve them, one must 'impose no burden beyond what is indispensable' (Acts 15:28). It is the council's urgent desire that every effort should henceforth be made toward the gradual realization of this goal in the various organizations and living activities of the church, especially by prayer and by fraternal dialogue on points of doctrine and the more pressing pastoral problems of our time" (UR, #18).

Without clarity on what is indispensable, there can be no assurance that we are not imposing unjustifiable obligations and demands on the partner churches. The only obligations and demands that are justifiable are the ones we hold before God as integral to the gospel. If they include more than the scriptures and the two creeds, we must explain how far they do extend—and why they do so—to our partners.

Rahner and Fries argue that each church could bring the day of reunion closer by discerning and declaring its ecumenical "bottom line," the conditions under which it would be willing to enter into unity with the others. "When establishing such conditions, each church would have the duty and responsibility—derived from the commandment of Jesus—to expand its own conditions no more than is clearly commanded by its own religious conviction of what is important to salvation" (9). Nothing beyond the necessary! Konrad Raiser agrees. He points out that ecclesiological discussion without a clear awareness of the fundamentals of faith only fosters further fragmentation. Such ecumenical dialogue only discovers more and more differences that seem to preclude reunion (Address).

Without clarity on the conditions it deems *essential* for church unity, a church becomes hesitant and dilatory. It fears the possibility of mistaking an integral element of faith for a dispensable element of its tradition, of surrendering some God-given portion of its heritage. Its uncertainty and confusion seem to justify delay and inaction. It does not know the next steps that it needs to take. Its official dialogues seem to uncover only more and more obstacles to unity (Dulles, Ecumenism, 22).

For instance, the "Common Declaration" of Archbishop Robert Runcie and Pope John Paul II names the Anglican–Roman Catholic division over the ordination of women a "difference in faith [which] reflects important ecclesiological differences...." Careful exegetical studies have concluded, however, that there is no biblical prohibition to ordaining women. Moreover, Roman Catholic theologians have raised cogent objections to the reasoning of *Inter Insigniores*, the 1976 document from the Congregation for the Doctrine of the Faith that sets forth the official position of the Roman Catholic Church. (A recent and significant critic is Peter Hünermann, the president of the Association of European Theologians; see Hebblethwaite, "Not") These factors make it hard to understand why the Common Declaration calls the ordination of women a "difference in faith."

A similiar problem appears in the response of the Vatican to the *Final Report* of ARCIC I (December 1991). The International Commission that submitted the report did not address the ordination of women directly. It held that "the principles upon which its doctrinal agreement rests are not affected by such ordinations; for it was concerned with the origin and nature of the ordained ministry and not with the question of who can or who cannot be ordained" (44). The Vatican answered, however, that decisions about who can be ordained reflect an understanding of "the nature of the sacrament of orders" and therefore the ordination of women requires a reexamination of the agreement which the commission claimed to reach (Response, 129).

Until the Roman Church is clear on what belongs to the integrity of the faith and what belongs to human traditions, the ordination of women will be church-dividing in fact, if not in theology.

The same lack of clarity drastically lessens the contribution that the new *Catechism of the Catholic Church* might have made to the church's ecumenical efforts. John Paul II maintains that the Catechism should support ecumenism by "showing carefully the content and wondrous harmony of the catholic faith" (*FD*, 5–6). Yet a key element of Roman Catholic ecumenical theology, the hierarchy of truths, is simply mentioned twice (Sections 90 and 234) and is not utilized as a structuring principle in the catechism. Though the text rightly presents the Trinity as the fundamental dogma in the hierarchy of truths (#234) and belief in the incarnation as "the distinctive sign of Christian faith" (#463), the catechism does not locate other truths of faith on a scale of importance relative to these two. Instead, it stresses their interconnected, organic character. The catechism's aim is to present "an organic synthesis of the essential and fundamental contents of Catholic doctrine, as regards both faith and morals..." (Section 11), as if the acceptance of one element logically required the acceptance of them all. As a result, the realm of the essential elements of a unity of faith appears much broader than it is.

Book One of the catechism is structured on the Apostles' Creed and Nicene Creed. This organizing principle has ecumenical potential. As Rahner and Fries have argued, these texts articulate the essentials of the Christian faith. Also, the project of the Faith and Order Commission of the World Council of Churches,

"Confessing the One Faith," begun in 1982, centers on the Nicene-Constantinopolitan Creed.

Yet the pain and damage caused by the divisions within the one church of Christ remain in the distant background of the catechism. Never does it affirm that the work of the Spirit among our Christian sisters and brothers can serve to build up the Roman Catholic Church (UR, #4). It grounds the apostolicity of the church almost exclusively in episcopal succession, not in teaching (Section 857 is an exception), and so mitigates the apostolicity of many Christian churches.

Characteristic of the catechism's spirit is that it never recalls the famous first sentence of GS: "The joys and the hopes, the griefs and the anxieties of the people of this age, especially those who are poor or in any way afflicted, these too are the joys and the hopes, the griefs and the anxieties of the followers of Christ." This signaled the desire to end the church's isolation from the world and to open dialogue with all people.

A church "intimately linked with humankind and its history" and eager to contribute to the unity that Jesus prayed for is not, however, the church that appears in the new catechism. It does not recall how much the church has gained from the experience of humanity and developments in the humanities and sciences (GS, #44). GS, #62 is cited once, but not its teaching on the role of culture and the sciences in evangelization; on the lawful freedom of inquiry, thought and expression in the church; on the difference between the substance of the deposit of faith and the manner of its expression.

This difference was axial to John XXIII's vision for Vatican II. In John Paul II's view, "The principal task entrusted to the council by Pope John XXIII was to guard and present better the precious deposit of Christian doctrine in order to make it more accessible to the Christian faithful and to all people of good will. For this reason the council was...to strive calmly to show the strength and beauty of the doctrine of the faith" (FD, 2).

But John XXIII opened the Council by declaring,

Our task is not merely to hoard this precious treasure, as though obsessed with the past, but to give ourselves eagerly and without fear to *the task that the present age demands of us* —and in so doing we will be faithful to what the Church has done in the last twenty centuries. So the main point of this Council will not be to debate this or that article of basic Church doctrine that has been repeatedly taught by the Fathers and theologians old and new and which we can take as read. You do not need a Council to do that. But starting from a renewed, serene and calm acceptance of the whole teaching of the Church in all its scope and detail as it is found in Trent and Vatican I, Christians and Catholics of apostolic spirit all the world over expect a leap [*balzo*] forward in doctrinal insight [*penetrazione*] and the education of consciences [*la formazione delle conscienze*] in ever great fidelity to authentic teaching. But this authentic doctrine *has to be studied and expounded in light of the research methods and the language [formulazione letteraria] of modern thought.* For the substance of the ancient deposit of faith is one thing, and the way in which it is presented is another (Hebblethwaite, Shepherd, 431-432; Emphases added).

This key purpose of Vatican II is not adequately reflected nor carried out in the new catechism. Consequently, ecumenists who try to meet the challenge posed by UR, #11 by discerning and utilizing the hierarchy of truths in the Roman Catholic tradition will have to defend their project. Its importance will be questioned. Its validity will be attacked as "ecumenism by reduction" by those who think that the "foundation of Christian faith" (UR, #11) is a minimum and not the maximum entailed in God's becoming human and revealing the mystery of God as Trinity. It will be seen as a desperate attempt to discover the lowest possible level of agreement acceptable to the churches, wherein each church's distinctive doctrines are either forgotten or negotiated away for the sake of reunion.

In discerning the content of the hierarchy of truths, Roman Catholic theologians will find it helpful to explore particular cases. For example, Hans Küng and Charles Curran have openly disagreed with certain official teachings of the Roman Catholic Church. Both men held professorships on "pontifical faculties" chartered by the Vatican. Both were removed from their teaching positions when they refused to change their positions. Küng no longer teaches on the Catholic faculty at Tübingen and Curran teaches at Perkins School of Theology at Southern Methodist University, instead of the Catholic University of America.

Yet neither Küng nor Curran was excommunicated. Nor were they threatened with excommunication during their correspondence and conversation with the Congregation for the Doctrine of the Faith. Nor were they removed from the priesthood and forbidden to preach and celebrate the sacrament of unity, the eucharist. Obviously, in the judgment of the Roman authorities, Küng and Curran remain within the basic unity of the faith held by the Catholic Church because they continue to preside at the primary sacrament of unity, the eucharist.

This consideration gathers additional significance in light of the fact that Küng denied the doctrine of Vatican I on infallibility. While the doctrine itself is defined and authoritative, Küng's continuing status as a priest despite his denial reveals that infallibility cannot belong to the foundation of the Christian faith, as the Catholic Church understands it. Infallibility is secondary and derivative in the sense that Karl Rahner has shown: it stems from the belief in God's eschatologically victorious salvation established in the world as a continuing historical presence (Rahner, Foundations, 384–387).

If Küng continues to preach in Roman Catholic churches and to celebrate the sacrament of the eucharist for which, John Paul II has declared, a unity of faith is required, then it is obvious that the Roman Catholic Church does not demand explicit acceptance of

Pastor Aeternus as a condition for intercommunion. The Church cannot demand a greater degree of doctrinal agreement from other communions than it does from its own members.

Unity Must Be Enacted

The unity in faith that already exists among the partner churches, that communion that is "certain yet imperfect" (Declaration, 672), has to be made more visible. It has to be embodied and enacted. At the moment the churches behave too much like spouses who say that they love one another, yet they spend little time together and never even hold hands to symbolize and deepen their bond. Until and unless the unity that exists between the churches is expressed not merely in words but in all the rituals and activities that go to realize the churches' mission and nature, the churches will be living a lie.

In marriages, the lack of a common life and physical contact is pathological. In the churches, their lack of cooperation and their continuing isolation from each other is deceptive. Their separateness tells them and the world that they do not share as much as they really do, that they are not united as closely as they really are. This is a massive anomaly. The trouble is that we are so used to it.

"By her relationship with Christ," says Vatican II, "the Church is a kind of sacrament or sign of intimate union with God, and of the unity of all humankind. She is also an instrument for the achievement of such union and unity" (LG, #1). The churches' continuing divisions make this sound like innocent idealism. What the church of Christ can be and do for a divided humanity is constantly hampered by its own inner rifts. This church does not look like the remedy but, instead, the reflection of the human propensity to conflict. Duprey suggests that the particular churches act too much like adolescents, maintaining their distinctive identities by stressing what differentiates them. They also mimic corporations in trying to get people to buy their version of Christianity and to solidify consumers' brand loyalty to their product.

As long as the churches keep the distance between them as wide as possible, they provide no model for unity amid diversity. They do not guide enemies into the kind of reconciliation that Bosnia, Northern Ireland, the Middle East, South Africa, and so many other places need so urgently. When the churches no longer insist that others must accept their own particularities as the price of unity, then the world—and even their own members —will find it easier to believe that Jesus comes from the one God and Father of us all (Jn 17:20).

Christians get complacent when their unity in faith is expressed merely in the words of agreed statements, but not in the rituals and activities of their own particular churches. Most Roman Catholics, Episcopalians, Lutherans, Methodists, Baptists, etc. are quite content with their isolation from each other. They live their discipleship within the borders of their church alone and get used to the notion that all the "riches of Christ" (UR, #4) can be found right there. They imagine that their church can answer the world's questions and meet the world's challenges all by itself.

They can escape these traps by taking the challenge of Lund seriously. Recall the "Word to the Churches" from the third world conference on Faith and Order (Lund, Sweden; 1952): "Should not our churches ask themselves...whether they should not act together in all matters except those in which deep differences of conviction compel them to act separately?" (Tomkins, 16). Keeping this question alive and acting upon the answers to it on every level of church life from local congregation and parish to national and international headquarters, the churches could begin to express the unity that exists among them.

Lund proposes that the churches cooperate with one another as much as possible, even in those areas that heretofore were used to reinforce their separate identities. Now the partner churches can and should develop and implement cooperative programs to prepare people for baptism, confirmation, marriage, and even ordination.

Joint programs for baptism and confirmation will reflect the meaning of these sacraments as initiation into the church of Christ. The churches do not exist in order to perpetuate themselves in their distinctiveness but to witness to the gospel and help to form people in the ways of discipleship. Joint programs can include particular segments where each tradition can educate its members in its distinctive doctrines and traditions. Then the students can come together again to share with each other what they have learned separately. Yes, the comparisons and contrasts may lead some students to change churches. That is a clear but necessary risk, if students are taught the truth of the one Church of Christ. Yet the same comparisons and contrasts will mean more informed and committed church members. Christians will be Roman Catholics, Episcopalians, Baptists, and Methodists not because they do not know any other church but because they do—and they have still chosen to make their religious home in their particular church.

Ecumenical education and formation programs for ministry and ordination, like the Colgate-Rochester Divinity School-Bexley Hall-Crozer Theological Seminary with some twenty denominations represented among its students, already exemplify a response to the challenge of Lund. Certainly, the ecumenical seminary experience is not always idyllic. Church differences mean that tensions are built into the common life. Seminar discussions can be difficult as students struggle to understand the terminology and outlook of fellow Christians of other churches. Common life and worship can be battlegrounds where the churches' differing traditions clash. Yet the unity of faith calls for this demanding preparation, so that the church's future leaders escape the illusion that their own church is sufficiently Christian all by itself or that it does not need the insight and experience of partner churches to be deeply faithful to its own vocation.

Joint programs to prepare people for ordination in the Roman Catholic Church would help to fulfill the summons of UR and the mandate of *Optatam Totius*, the decree on priestly formation of Vatican II. UR, #9 and #10 do not precisely envision these joint educational ventures but they declare, "We must come to understand the outlook of our separated brothers [and sisters]" (#9) and "Instruction in sacred theology and other branches of knowledge...must also be presented from an ecumenical point of view, so that at every point they may more accurately correspond with the facts of the case" (#10). *Optatam Totius*, #16 calls for future priests to be "led to a more adequate understanding of the Churches and ecclesial communities separated from the Roman, Apostolic See. Thus the students can contribute to the restoration of unity among all Christians...." Where can these goals be more effectively and efficiently realized than in an ecumenical setting, sharing life with separated sisters and brothers?

Models for cooperative seminary programs now exist in the United States, where a consortium serves a group of religious orders. The Washington Theological Consortium, the Catholic Theological Union in Chicago, and the Graduate Theological Union in Berkeley are trailblazers here. In these situations, each religious order maintains its own residence. Here its students are formed in the traditions of spirituality and community that reflect the order's charism and mission. But each order contributes professors to the faculty and administration of the consortium. Its students study and work with students from the other orders. Unity is expressed in the joint studies set down by curriculum requirements and diversity is preserved in the separate residences. The order's uniquenesses enrich the common life of the seminar room and dining hall.

The models for cooperative seminary education already exist and have proven their worth. The pragmatic benefits are obvious: by pooling resources, the students for each order receive the quality of education that no single order could provide by itself. The imperative implicit in Lund's question calls for the scope of these programs to be expanded beyond religious orders to include other Christian denominations.

There should be cooperative programs to prepare bishops, as well as priests and ministers, in the churches. As bishops struggle to minister to their people, many have found themselves drawn to

their counterparts from other Christian churches in the same territory. This commonality is not sheer coincidence. Their close relationships testify to the experiences, motivations, and perspectives
that many in the episcopacy already share. It witnesses to their
unity of faith.

For years the Roman Catholic Church in the United States
has conducted programs to prepare new bishops for their ministry.
Recently, the Episcopal Church has begun its own similiar program, the College of Bishops, which convened for the first time at
the General Theological Seminary in February 1994. A joint program for Roman Catholic and Episcopal bishops, however, could
draw on the best resource people in both churches. Separate program segments could be designed to cover canonical issues particular to each church.

Such cooperative formation programs are even more necessary, now that an ecumenical attitude and commitment seem to be
less important in choosing bishops in the Roman Church. On an
apparently official list of twelve detailed criteria for episcopal candidates, "an ecumenical attitude" is less important than "convinced and faithful adherence to the teaching and magisterium of
the church...especially the transmission of life according to the
teaching of *Humanae Vitae* and...*Familiaris Consortio...*"
(Hebblethwaite, Secret, 14).

Finally, and most importantly, structures of mutual accountability are needed to actualize the real though imperfect communion in Jesus Christ that now exists among the churches. Imperfect
though it is, this communion must be canonically and liturgically
enacted. Without structures of mutual accountability, the churches
are not living out the unity that is theirs, even though it is not yet
complete and fully visible. Without structures of mutual accountability, the churches behave like people who say, "I love you," but
do absolutely nothing to prove that statement. Now the churches
look all too much like those people, acknowledging their unity in
words but doing too little to make that unity visible and effective in
their inner lives.

Structures of mutual accountability would foster (and perhaps even require by covenant) the consultation of churches with each other before taking any major initiative or making any major declaration. For instance, if the Roman Church wishes to promote a particular policy at a United Nations Conference on World Hunger and, according to its agreement to work within structures of mutual accountability, consults its partners well in advance, the partners might refine the proposal and add their hands and voices to the effort. The initiative then has a greater chance of success.

Yet the fundamental reason for establishing and using structures of mutual accountability is not their pragmatic benefits. Mutual understanding among the churches will grow by means of these structures. If John Paul II had consulted with other churches before issuing *Ordinatio Sacerdotalis* in May 1994, its tone might have been more irenic and its content more persuasive. If he had consulted other churches before issuing *Veritatis Splendor* in the fall of 1993, the encyclical might not have been taken so readily as a rationale for some future purge of "dissenting" Catholic moral theologians. Structures of mutual accountability might have drawn other churches too into critical reflection and cooperation on the moral climate of the contemporary world. If wide Christian consultation had been used to prepare the May 1992 letter from the Congregation for the Doctrine of the Faith on *Some Aspects of the Church Understood as Communion*, it might not have been taken as a major ecumenical setback and the later clarifications by Cardinal Ratzinger would have been unnecessary. If structures of acountability had been used to prepare the official Vatican response to the Final Report of ARCIC I, that response would likely have been more positive and theologically competent.

Denominational particularities can remain in place along with structures of mutual accountability. They would, however, make a certain communion of communions operative and visible long before the fullness of communion can be realized. They would enact the unity of faith without pushing churches into a visible corporate unity before they are prepared. Nor would structures of mutual accountability prevent one church from acting or speaking on its own, if it were convinced that its fidelity to Christ demanded it. Accountability is not equivalent to giving another church veto power over the judgments of one's own.

Maintain the Dialogues

The structures of mutual accountability create a new context and establish a new purpose for the bi-lateral and multi-lateral dialogues. These dialogues alone cannot carry the churches to the full, visible unity that is the goal of the ecumenical movement. Raiser claims that the dialogues' usefulness on that score is over, and there is abundant evidence to support his claim. The theologians who carry on the dialogues can always find something more to disagree about, and, as Henry Chadwick has observed, many theologians are terrified by the prospect of agreement!

Yet the dialogues must continue. Any future church unity requires their support. Recall that the Rahner–Fries proposal stipulates continuing dialogue even after church unity has been secured. These dialogues keep theological differences, variations in styles of liturgy and devotion, and doctrinal differences that are more remote from the foundation of Christian faith from becoming church-dividing once again (Raiser, Paradigm,17).

The dialogues must continue also because they are the means by which the churches keep faith with their ancestors and honor the memory of their own heroes and martyrs, as they move more deeply into the one visible church of Christ. Dulles is right: no secure unity can be bought at the cost of the churches' surrendering their God-given gifts and consigning their divinely-guided histories to ecumenical oblivion. For example, Lutherans have to know that Catholics understand and accept "justification by faith alone" and that they are grateful that Lutheranism has kept this cardinal tenet of the gospel at the forefront of Christian consciousness. Catholics have to know that Anglicans accept the real presence of Christ in the eucharist, despite their differences in eucharistic devotion.

Anglicans have to know that other Christians accept that Christ's authority properly resides in the the "historic episcopate locally adapted," as well as in scripture and the creeds.

The continuing dialogues are the means for reaching these necessary mutual understandings and their resulting agreed statements cast them in public, permanent form.

Papal Primacy: From Obstacle to Opportunity

The doctrine of papal primacy has loomed as an enduring and seemingly intractable obstacle on the pilgrimage toward unity. So the statement that "The pope, as we well know, is undoubtedly the gravest obstacle in the path of ecumenism," is remarkable not for its content but for the one who said it, Paul VI himself in an address to the Secretariat for Promoting Christian Unity. He continued by posing the question of this section: "What shall we say?" (Tillard, 18). What, indeed?

The adamant, peremptory, and unnuanced assertions of the pope's prerogatives march across the page of the dogmatic constitution *Pastor Bonus* (1870). The canon to Chapter 3, "On the Power and Rationale for the Primacy of the Roman Pontiff," says

> And so if anyone should say that the Roman Pontiff has in some way the duty of oversight and direction but not the full and supreme power of jurisdiction over the whole Church not only in matters pertaining to faith and morals but also in matters which pertain to the discipline and governance of the Churches spread throughout the whole world; or that he has only the principal part but not the full plenitude of this supreme power or that his power is not ordinary and immediate, whether over all and each of the Churches or over all and each of the pastors and faithful; let that one be anathema (DS 3064; translation mine).

Since papal primacy is now irreformable and binding Roman Catholic doctrine defined by Vatican I and confirmed by Pius IX, it seems an impenetrable barrier to reunion of the Church of Christ. Surely, Cuthbert Butler was prescient when he wrote, "Though at the time of the Council it was the infallibility [sic] that raised the greatest storms...I cannot help thinking that the matter of the primacy...in reality presents much greater difficulties to non-Catholics of all kinds, much greater obstacles to that united Christendom in communion with the Apostolic See of Rome and its bishop..." (Butler, 330).

Yet doctrines must be understood in their context. The context for the doctrine of primacy is the Constitution *Pastor Aeternus*. Its context, in turn, is formed by the conciliar schemas, discussions, debates, and the *relatio* (the official clarification and explanation) of the text given at the council itself. The context of Vatican I as a whole was the sense of crisis that had seized many of the leading churchmen of the day—including Pope Pius IX.

His bull of June 29, 1868 which convoked the council expresses the sense of crisis in dramatic terms:

> It is at this time evident and manifest to all men in how horrible a tempest the Church is now tossed, and with what vast evils civil society is afflicted...not only our holy religion but human society itself is plunged in an unspeakable state of disorder and suffering. Wherefore we have judged it to be opportune to bring together...a General Council...(Butler, 69).

As many of the church's leaders conceived it, the fundamental purpose of Vatican I was to give the church the weapon it needed to cope with the most serious challenges it had ever faced. The church, in their view, was under siege. If it buckled under the onslaught of liberalism, secularism, atheism, and indifferentism, western civilization (to their minds, the only civilization worthy of the name!) would collapse along with it. For the majority of the bishops at Vatican I, de Maistre had it exactly right: "No public morals or national character without religion, no European religion without Christianity, no Christianity without Catholicism, no Catholicism without the Pope, and no Pope without the supremacy that belongs to him" (Tillard, 21).

In the throes of an imminently threatening and massive crisis, careful deliberation and concern for long-range consequences can look like luxuries. Weapons to repel the threat are wanted as soon as possible. This was the mentality of the majority at Vatican I. *Pastor Aeternus* was crafted in great part by fearful and impatient men.

Soon after the council opened on December 8, 1869, it adopted an agenda. The first order of business was to clarify and affirm Catholic teaching on faith, revelation, and reason against the most influential errors of the day, such as rationalism and fideism. Accordingly, months of work led to the promulgation of the dogmatic constitution *Dei Filius* on April 24, 1870.

On January 21, however, the council fathers had been given a draft of their second order of business, a dogmatic constitution on the Church of Christ (*De Ecclesia Christi*). This schema contained fifteen chapters and twenty-one canons. Only Chapters 11 and 12 dealt with the papacy.

As the discussion of this draft wore on, Cardinal Henry Manning from England began to worry. Two days after the council had been announced (June 26, 1867), he and another bishop, Senestrey of Ratisbon (Regensburg), had stood by the pope's throne to make a solemn vow to do all they could to secure a dogmatic definition of papal infallibility from the council. Manning now feared that if the agreed order of topics were followed, the council could end before producing such a definition. (Tensions in Europe were mounting and the Franco-Prussian war did break out on July 19, 1870, one day after the final vote and ratification of *Pastor Aeternus*.) So Manning and his allies swung into action.

Led by Manning and Senestrey, over two hundred bishops petitioned the council presidents to change the order of topics. They wanted Chapters 11 and 12 on the papacy removed from the schema on the church and prepared as a separate document. This new constitution would then be taken up by the council immediately after approval of *Dei Filius*. The council presidents denied the request, so Manning's group persuaded Pius IX himself to intervene. As a result, the presidents announced on April 29 that discussion would soon begin on the schema *De Summo Pontifice* (Butler, 297–299).

The bishops of the minority included some of the most capable minds of the church, like Rauscher of Vienna, Dupanloup of Orleans, Kettler of Mainz, and Kenrick of St. Louis. They were stunned by this change in the council's process. Not only did it negate the procedural agreements that had been made but it also created severe theological and practical problems.

How, they asked, can we discuss and define the role of the pope when we are not yet clear on the elements which form the context for a proper understanding of the papacy: the mystery of the church and its fundamental purpose in the world, the institution of the episcopate, the power and role of councils in the church, and the other dogmas that have a bearing on this matter (Hennesey, 223; Tillard, 130–131)? In the minority's view, the new order of topics would inevitably produce an unbalanced definition of the pope's role.

They also prophetically argued that the change would hinder evangelism and ecumenism, although they did not use that terminology. When the council had first been announced, overtures had been made to Protestants and Orthodox but they had been inept overtures—and so they were rejected (Butler, 74–76). Yet there remained ecumenically sensitive bishops among the minority who still hoped that Vatican I might advance the cause of Christian unity. The schema on the papacy, however, threatened to destroy their hopes. As Bishop Wiery from Austria said, the document would probably provoke other Christians to charge, "You Catholics, papists, you look for your savior at Rome and not from heaven; you expect salvation from the Pope and not from Christ" (Granfield, 39).

The majority remained unpersuaded and undeterred by these considerations. Convinced of their sole possession of the truth, they argued that it was their task as bishops to teach it. If papal primacy meant the full, ordinary, immediate, universal, and properly episcopal jurisdiction of the pope, then the council must declare it clearly and firmly. The bishops must leave it to God to change the hearts and minds of Protestants and Orthodox who could not now accept this divine truth. In the meantime, said Bishop Zinelli, the *relator* (or official spokesman for the drafting committee), we should pray for them and define the truth without fear (Butler, 344).

For the majority, defining the truth meant stating it boldly and baldly, not necessarily presenting it in as full and as persuasive a context as possible. To do that would have required extensive discussions on the nature and mission of the church. These would have delayed and possibly prevented a definition on the papacy, a possibility that was intolerable to the majority.

The minority developed a fallback position: let us formulate *Pastor Aeternus* with the nuances, qualifications, and limits on papal power that all of us, majority and minority, know about and agree upon. Now all power, including the pope's, is shaped and limited by its purpose. The power of the pope exists to build up the church (a notion drawn from 2 Cor 10:8 and used by Zinelli in his *relatio*) and to foster its unity (Granfield, 62). It is also limited by natural and divine law, a point also made by Zinelli. Papal power is normally to be exercised according to the canons. It cannot be used to mitigate, much less to abolish, other elements of the church which exist *iure divino*, by God's decree: the scriptures, the episcopate, tradition. So, for example, primacy does not mean that the pope has the right to interfere with the proper exercise of a bishop's jurisdiction in his own diocese.

The majority, however, resisted proposals to include these limitations in the text of *Pastor Aeternus*. Their reason was strategic, not theological. They saw their church under attack and their civilization threatened. So, they said, there are certainly limits and qualifications to the pope's jurisdiction. These are well known to us, so well known that they need not be put into the text itself. Nor should they be put into the text. If we state the limits, our document will be perceived as a weakening of the pope's power precisely when that power has to be strengthened as a bulwark for our embattled church and culture (Tillard, 28, 131; Granfield, 41–42). We must state the truth simply and clearly: papal primacy means the full, ordinary, immediate, universal, and properly episcopal jurisdiction. If we do not, we will have weakened what most needs to be strengthened.

The final vote and ratification of *Pastor Aeternus* was set for July 18, 1870. On the evening of July 15, a delegation from the minority went to Pius IX. They pleaded with him for modifications in the canon of the third chapter of the Constitution (quoted above) that would free them to vote for it in good conscience. Kettler of Mainz even fell to his knees before the pope with tears in his eyes: "Good Father, save us, and save the church of God." Pius was unwilling to override the will of the majority that was clear by now and so he refused (Butler, 406–407).

Many of the minority bishops got permission to leave Rome before the final vote, hoping that their absence would produce at least the appearance of unanimity. They nearly succeeded. The final count was 535 in favor, 2 opposed (one of which was cast by the bishop of Little Rock, Arkansas).

Pastor Aeternus can, nonetheless, be transformed from an obstacle into an ecumenical opportunity. The pope and the bishops could now undertake a public and official re-examination of the meaning and limits of papal primacy in order to advance the cause of reunion. In this effort, they could draw upon the theological consensus on the meaning of primacy as it has been developed by authors like Tillard and Granfield. They could thereby offer to the entire church of Christ a contextualized and nuanced intepretation of primacy which the majority and the minority alike agreed upon at Vatican I.

This work would show that the power of the pope, according to the most orthodox Roman Catholic teaching, exists ad *aedifica-*

tionem Ecclesiae non ad destructionem, for the building up and not the tearing down of the church. The pope and the bishops could remind the entire church that Vatican I understood "plenary" and "supreme" power to mean that it can be limited by natural and divine law, but not by any higher human power (a point made by Bishop Zinelli in his explanation to the council fathers before the final vote). Papal power is termed "ordinary" not as opposed to extraordinary but in the canonical sense, that is, power that is not delegated from another. As "immediate," papal power can be exercised, if necessary, without having to go through intermediaries. It does not mean *carte blanche* for the pope to intervene in the routine and orderly administration of a diocese by its bishop. Finally, this power is truly episcopal, for it is the bishop of Rome who exercises it for the sake of the unity of the church.

This initiative would eviscerate the theologically untenable, ultramontane interpretations of *Pastor Aeternus* that still create so many misunderstandings, even among Roman Catholics. At the same time, it would be an effective response to many non-Catholic Christians who ask why the church, as Catholics understand it, requires papal primacy and how primacy can serve the cause of unity in faith (Tillard, 225, n.76).

The Roman Catholic Church would then stand before the entire church of Christ in eagerness to discern and teach the whole truth about the role of the pope, in eagerness to remove as much as possible of that obstacle which Paul VI recognized as the main one in ecumenism. Then what he said of the Church of England might be seen as equally true for all the churches: "There will be no seeking to lessen the legitimate prestige and the worthy patrimony of piety and usage proper to the Anglican Church when the Roman Catholic Church...is able to embrace her ever beloved sister in the one authentic communion of the family of Christ..." (Witmer, 54–55). The papacy would then be the servant of unity—not the illusory unity of conformity but the authentic unity of communion.

The appropriate studies and subsequent declaration then

have to be accompanied by action. Papal primacy must be exercised to illustrate and demonstrate its true meaning and effectiveness as a sign and promoter of unity. A guiding principle in every primatial initiative would now have to be the principle drawn from the first council held in Jerusalem and binding on the church of the present: to impose no burden beyond what is necessary.

The pope could immediately call for the necessary changes in canon law that return more power and initiative to episcopal conferences. This change would attract the Anglican Communion and the Orthodox churches who rightly treasure their traditions of synodical governance and surely will accept no primacy that does not respect those traditions as well.

Greater diversity in matters that are important but do not require uniformity in the church will surely result. It is likely, for instance, that bishops in regions where the shortage of priests has deprived their people of acess to the eucharist will quickly decide to rectify this by ordaining married men, the "viri probati." (The bishops of Indonesia and northwestern Canada have already asked and been denied permission from Rome for this. Archbishop Rembert Weakland of Milwaukee was also rebuffed when he made a similiar initiative). The new range of decision-making power will enact and acknowledge the rights and responsibilities of bishops as the shepherds of their dioceses.

"Without a doubt there have been misguided developments in both theology and practice where the primacy is concerned..." (Ratzinger, Anglican, 77–78) and reform of the primacy should include a change in the manner of choosing and installing bishops. Welcoming a new bishop into the college of bishops belongs to the papal role and duty, since the pope is head of the college (LG, #22). So primacy would entail papal veto power over certain candidates, though this power should not be exercised without extensive consultation. But the appointment of bishops is not a papal prerogative; it is a relatively recent development in the long history of the church. The primacy could be attractive to other Christians, especially Anglicans and Orthodox, if the pope were to lead the church in a reinvigoration of the more traditional ways of choosing bishops, ways that allowed the people a voice in selecting who was to serve them as bishop.

Structuring consultation and collaboration in the exercise of primacy will lead to substantial changes in the church, but the hardships have to be suffered for the sake of truth and for the credibility of the gospel. Declarations and policies of the pope must be seen more clearly as necessary to protect the gospel from misappropriation.

For instance, the 1976 declaration of the Congregation for the Doctrine of the Faith, *Inter Insigniores*, states the position of the Roman Catholic Church on the admission of women to holy orders. This statement, however, has been consistently and severely criticized for the weakness of its arguments (Stuhlmueller; Swidler). Yet the position continues to be maintained as if it were definitive, and it has even become something of a litmus test for prospective bishops (Hebblethwaite, Secret, 14).

The weakness of the arguments, plus Rome's persistence in enforcing the policy by means of power instead of theological reasoning, fuels suspicion that it is not the gospel but patriarchy that stands behind the position. When persuasive counter-arguments are ignored, many can be forgiven for seeing primacy being exercised here not to defend the faith and promote the unity of the church but to resist certain developments in western culture. In their view, what stands behind *Inter Insigniores* is not the apostolic faith but, rather, a conviction that pressure for women's ordination stems from movements that destabilize the family by encouraging women to step out of their roles as wife, mother, and homemaker.

The whole church of Christ has had to live too long with the consequences of *Pastor Aeternus* with its peremptory, unqualified language. While Vatican II attempted to complete the work left unfinished by the premature closure of Vatican I by placing primacy within the context of episcopal collegiality, many inside and outside the church still consider the papal ministry as a religious dictatorship. The unity of the churches can dawn only when this misunderstanding is laid to rest by a more accurate understanding and a reformed practice of primacy.

No More Reordinations

When a priest of the Anglican Communion is accepted for priestly ministry in the Roman Catholic Church, he is absolutely "reordained"—as if his previous ordination had no sacramental effect whatsoever. This policy reflects the judgment of Pope Leo XIII in *Apostolicae Curae* (1896) that Anglican orders are "absolutely null and utterly void." Now, 98 years after that verdict, the Roman Catholic Church has many reasons to change its policy, even without a full-scale reversal of *Apostolicae Curae*. After appropriate consultation, the pope could end the policy of absolutely ordaining and institute conditional ordinations for Anglicans and perhaps for certain others as well.

The agreed statement of the ARC–USA, "Anglican Orders: The Dialogue's Evolving Context," details the reasons in support of reopening the issue of Anglican orders. It argues that there is now a new context for examining this question. While Leo XIII's verdict was defensible in light of the historical evidence and theological reasoning available to him, ARC–USA has shown that many other factors have developed since 1896 to change the *status quaestionis*. Added to the ARC study should be the book of George Tavard, *A Review of Anglican Orders: The Problem and the Solution*, which effectively puts the burden of proof on those who would defend *Apostolicae Curae* as adequate justification for the policy of absolute ordinations today.

So there are ample grounds for holding that a new context for the validity question calls for a re-examination of the judgment of 1896. Pending the outcome of this re-examination and in light of the affirmation of Vatican II that the rituals of even the "brethren divided from us...can truly engender a life of grace, and can rightly be described as capable of providing access to the community of salvation" (UR, #3), no Anglican priest should henceforth be absolutely reordained as a Roman Catholic priest. This change of policy would reflect more accurately the new context. It would also manifest the long overdue respect for the ministry and devotion of these priests during the years of their service in the Anglican Communion.

Conclusion

It is time for the Roman Catholic Church to prove that it is committed to church unity, not just to ecumenical dialogue.

There are initiatives that the Roman Catholic Church can and should now undertake on its own to make its ecumenical commitments credible and effective. Its words have been many, frequent, and eloquent. Most recently: "The ecumenical movement is a grace of God, given by the Father in answer to the prayer of Jesus and the supplication of the Church inspired by the Holy Spirit" (Directory, #22). "This unity which of its very nature requires full visible communion of all Christians is the ultimate goal of the ecumenical movement" (Directory, #20).

Now the question is: How will the Roman Catholic Church translate its words into deeds? Will it show its ecumenical partners how much it is willing to suffer and risk that all may be one? Will it now make those changes necessary for the unity of the churches, so that the light of the gospel may shine more fully on the world that needs a heart and soul for its unity so desperately?

> O God the Father of our Lord Jesus Christ, our only Savior, the Prince of Peace: Give us grace seriously to lay to heart the great dangers we are in by our unhappy divisions; take away all hatred and prejudice, and whatever else may hinder us from godly union and concord; that, as there is but one Body and one Spirit, one hope of our calling, one Lord, one Faith, one Baptism, one God and Father of us all, so we may be all of one heart and of one soul, united in one holy bond of truth and

peace, of faith and charity, and may with one mind and one mouth glorify *thee*; through Jesus Christ our Lord. Amen.

"For the Unity of the Church,"
Book of Common Prayer

Works Cited

Abbott, Walter M. and Gallagher, Joseph , eds., *The Documents of Vatican* II. New York: America, 1966.

Anglican-Roman Catholic Consultation in the United States. "Anglican Orders: The Dialogue's Evolving Context." *Origins* 20.9 (July 19, 1990), 136–146.

_____ "ARC–USA Agreed Statement on the Lambeth and Vatican Responses to ARCIC-I." *One in Christ* 29.3 (1993), 260–268.

Anglican–Roman Catholic International Commission. *The Final Report*. Cincinnati: Forward Movement, 1982.

"Appendix B: The Notion of 'Hierarchy of Truths'—An Ecumenical Interpretation," 285–293. Sixth Report of the Joint Working Group Between the Roman Catholic Church and the World Council of Churches. *One in Christ* 27.3 (1991), 246–293.

Archbishop Robert Runcie and Pope John Paul II, "Common Declaration" (October 2, 1989). *Catholic International* 2.14 (July 15–31, 1991), 671–672.

Aubert, Roger. "Aspects Divers du Neo-thomisme sous le Pontificat de Leon XIII." *Aspetti della Cultura cattolica nell'eta di Leone XIII*. Ed. Giuseppe Rossini. Rome: Edizioni 5 Lune, 1961, 133–227.

Bird, David John. *"The Anglican Communion occupies a special place": An Examination of the Background, Development and Reception in the Roman Catholic Church of the Text on the Special Place of the Anglican Communion in "Unitatis Redintegratio."* Ann Arbor: University Microfilms, 1987.

Bonn Agreement, 1931. *Growth in Agreement. Reports and Agreed Statements of Ecumenical Conversations on a World Level.* Ed. Harding Meyer and Lukas Vischer. New York: Paulist, 1984, 37–38.

Butler, Cuthbert. *The Vatican Council 1869–1870.* 1930. Ed. Christopher Butler. Westminster: Newman, 1962.

Catechism of the Catholic Church. Liguori: Liguori Publications, 1994; cited by paragraph numbers.

Chadwick, Henry. Remarks at National Consultation on Ecclesiology, sponsored by the Standing Committee on Ecumenical Relations of the Episcopal Church, October 18, 1993, Riverdale, New York.

Colella, Pasquale. "Considerations on the nomination of Bishops in Current Canon Law." Trans. John Bowden. *Collegiality Put to the Test.* Concilium 1990/4. Ed. James Provost and Knut Walf. London: SCM, 1990, 98–103.

Confessing the One Faith. An Ecumenical Explication of the Apostolic Faith as it is Confessed in the Nicene-Constantinopolitan Creed (381). Faith and Order Paper No. 153. Geneva: WCC, 1991.

Congregation for the Doctrine of the Faith. "Declaration in Defense of the Catholic Doctrine Against Certain Errors of the Present Day [*Mysterium Ecclesiae*]." *Origins* 3.7 (July 19, 1973), 97, 99–100, 110–112.

———— "Some Aspects of the Church Understood as Communion." *Origins* 22.7 (June 25, 1992), 108–111. Latin text: *L'Osservatore Romano* 132.138 (June 15–16, 1992), 7–8.

Denzinger, H.J.D. and Schönmetzer, ed. *Echiridion symbolorum, definitionum et declarationum de rebus fidei et moribus.* 33rd ed. Barcelona: Herder, 1965.

DiNoia, J.A. "Magisterium: Unity and Substance." Unpublished paper to appear in volume of studies on the Lutheran-Episcopal "Concordat of Agreement."

Directory for the Application of Principles and Norms of Ecumenism, Pontifical Council for Promoting Christian Unity. Catholic International 4.8 (August 1993), 351–399.

Ditmanson, Harold. "Presentation on Thesis #4b," unpublished paper for "Free Conference" sponsored by Division of

Theological Studies of the Lutheran Council in the U.S.A., Techny, Illinois, April 16–18, 1985.

Dulles, Avery. "Catholicism and American Culture: The Uneasy Dialogue." *America* January 27, 1990), 54–59.

———— "Ecumenical Strategies for a Pluralistic Age." *The Resilient Church*. Garden City: Doubleday, 1977, 173–190.

———— "Ecumenism Without Illusions: A Catholic Perspective." *First Things* (June–July 1990), 20–25.

———— "Paths to Doctrinal Agreement: Ten Theses."Theological Studies 47 (1986): 32–47. Reprinted as "Ecumenism and the Search for Doctrinal Agreement" in *The Reshaping of Catholicism*. San Francisco: Harper and Row, 1988, 227–245.

———— "Rethinking the Mission of the Church." *The Resilient Church*. Garden City: Doubleday, 1977, 9–28.

———— *The Catholicity of the Church*. 1985. Oxford: Oxford University Press, 1987.

———— "The Critique of Modernity and the Hartford Appeal."*The Resilient Church*. Garden City: Doubleday, 1977, 63–91.

Dunne, John S. *The City of the Gods. A Study in Myth and Mortality*. New York: Macmillan, 1965.

Duprey, Pierre. "Fundamental Consensus and Church Fellowship. A Roman Catholic Perspective," *In Search of Christian Unity. Basic Consensus/Basic Differences*. Ed. Joseph A. Burgess. Minneapolis: Fortress Press, 1991, 138–147.

"Ecumenical Chill." *Time* (March 11, 1985), 59.

Empie, Paul C. and Murphy, T. Austin. *Papal Primacy and the Universal Church*. Lutherans and Catholics in Dialogue V. Minneapolis: Augsburg, 1974.

Fries, Heinrich. "Die Thesen von Fries und Rahner und ihre Wirkungsgeschichte." *Theologische Quartalschrift* 166 (1986), 302–312.

———— "Thesis II." Paper given at "Free Conference" sponsored by Division of Theological Studies of the Lutheran Council in the U.S.A., Techny, Illinois, April 16–18, 1985.

Granfield, Patrick. *The Limits of the Papacy*. New York: Crossroad, 1987.

Greeley, Andrew and William McManus. *Catholic Contributions: Sociology and Policy*. Chicago: Thomas More, 1987.

Hebblethwaite, Peter. "'Secret' criteria set bishops' appointments." *National Catholic Reporter* 30.14 (February 4, 1994), 14.

_____ "John Paul II." *Modern Catholicism. Vatican II and After*. Ed. Adrian Hastings. New York: Oxford, 1991, 447–456.

_____ "Not the last word." *Tablet* 248.8014 (March 12,1994), 332–334.

_____ *Paul VI. The First Modern Pope*. New York: Paulist, 1993.

_____ *Pope John XXIII. Shepherd of the Modern World*. Garden City: Doubleday, 1985.

Hennesey, James. *The First Council of the Vatican: The American Experience*. New York: Herder and Herder, 1963.

John Paul II, "Address to the Delegations from Other Christian Churches (October 22 1978)." *John Paul II: Addresses and Homilies on Ecumenism, 1978–1980*. Ed. Tom Stransky and John F. Hotchkin. Washington: USCC Publications, 1981.

_____ Apostolic Constitution *Fidei Depositum* on the Publication of the Catechism of the Catholic Church in *Catechism of the Catholic Church*. Liguori: Liguori Publications, 1994, 1–6.

_____ "Pope John Paul II's Welcome." *One in Christ* 16 (1980/4), 341–342.

Joint Statement by Pope Paul VI and Archbishop Michael Ramsey of Canterbury, Rome (March 24, 1966). *Catholic International* 2.14 (July 15–31, 1991), 669.

Kasper, Walter. "Basic Consensus and Church Fellowship: The status of the ecumenical dialogue between the Roman Catholic and the Evangelical Lutheran Churches." *In Search of Christian Unity. Basic Consensus/Basic Differences*. Ed. Joseph A. Burgess. Minneapolis: Fortress, 1991, 21–44.

Lonergan, Bernard J.F. "The Transition from a Classicist World-

View to Historical Mindedness." *A Second Collection*. Ed. William F.J. Ryan and Bernard J. Tyrrell. Philadelphia: Westminster, 1974, 1–9.

———— "Theology in Its New Context." *A Second Collection*. Ed. William F.J. Ryan and Bernard J. Tyrrell. Philadelphia: Westminster, 1974, 55–67.

"Mexican ecumenical agreement signed." *Christian Century* 111.5 (February 16, 1994), 163

National Conference of Catholic Bishops. "Stewardship: A Disciple's Response." *Origins* 22.27 (December 17, 1992), 457, 459–471.

Nichols, Aidan. "'Einigung de Kirchen': an ecumenical controversy." *One in Christ*. 21.2 (1985), 139–166.

Nilson, Jon. "Aquinas in America." *Perspectives* 20.1 (Spring 1990), 21–31.

———— "Papal Primacy—from obstacle to opportunity." *Ecumenical Trends* 20.9 (October 1991), 131–134.

———— "Unity of the Churches: Actual Possibility or Eschatological Actuality?" *Philosophy and Theology* 8.1 (Autumn 1993), 3–23.

"No pacts, no deals in talks with Anglicans." *Tablet* 247:7959 (February 20, 1993), 255.

Official Response by the Holy See to the Final Report of the First Anglican-Roman Catholic International Commission. *Catholic International* 3.3 (February 1–14, 1992), 125–130.

Ols, Daniel. "Scorciatoie ecumeniche [Ecumenical Shortcuts]." Trans. John F. Hotchkin. *L'Osservatore Romano* CXXV.47 (February 25–26 1985), 1.

Orsy, Ladislas. "Towards Christian Unity Through the *Kenosis* of the Churches." *Ecumenical Trends* 22.7 (July–August 1993), 6/110–10/114.

Paul VI. "Remarks at Canonization of Forty Martyrs." [October 25, 1970] *Called to Full Unity: documents on Anglican-Roman Catholic relations 1966–1983*. Ed. Joseph W. Witmer and J. Robert Wright. Washington: United States Catholic Conference, 1986, 54–55.

Rahner, Karl and Fries, Heinrich. *Einigung der Kirchen —reale Möglichkeit.* Mit einer Bilanz 'Zustimmung und Kritik' von Heinrich Fries. Special edition of Quaestiones Disputatae, 100. Freiburg im Breisgau: Herder, 1985.

_____ *Unity of the Churches. An Actual Possibility.* 1983. Trans. Ruth C.L. Gritsch and Erik W. Gritsch. New York: Paulist, 1985.

Rahner, Karl. "A Hierarchy of Truths." *Theological Investigations,* vol. 21. Trans. Hugh M. Riley. New York: Crossroad, 1988, 162–167.

_____ "Aspects of European Theology," *Theological Investigations,* vol. 21. Trans. Hugh M. Riley. New York: Crossroad, 1988, 78–98.

_____ *Foundations of Christian Faith.* Trans. William V. Dych. New York: Seabury, 1978.

_____ *On Heresy.* Trans. W.J. O'Hara. *Quaestiones Disputatae,* 11. New York: Herder and Herder, 1964.

_____ "On the Situation of Faith." *Theological Investigations,* vol. 20. Trans. Edward Quinn. New York: Crossroad, 1981, 13–32.

_____ "Pluralism in Theology and the Unity of the Creed in the Church." *Theological Investigations,* vol. 11. Trans. David Bourke. New York: Seabury, 1974, 3–23.

_____ "Prayer for Reunion." Trans. Elliot Junger. *Prayers for a Lifetime.* Ed. Albert Raffeldt. New York: Crossroad, 1985, 164–165.

_____ "Reflections on Methodology in Theology." *Theological Investigations,* vol. 11. Trans. David Bourke. New York: Seabury, 1974, 68–114.

_____ "What is a Dogmatic Statement?" *Theological Investigations,* vol. 5. Trans. Karl-H. Kruger. New York: Seabury, 1966, 42–66.

Raiser, Konrad. Address to National Consultation on Ecclesiology, sponsored by the Standing Committee on Ecumenical Relations of the Episcopal Church, October 18, 1993, Riverdale, New York.

———— *Ecumenism in Transition. A Paradigm Shift in the Ecumenical Movement?* Trans. Tony Coates. Geneva: WCC, 1991

———— "What Future for Ecumenical Dialogues?" report of his speech, Rome, June 4, 1993. *Centro* (Newsletter of the Anglican Centre in Rome) 1.2 (July 1993)

Ratzinger, Joseph. "Anglican-Catholic dialogue: Its problems and hopes." *Church, Ecumenism & Politics. New Essays in Ecclesiology.* Trans. Frideswide Sandemann. New York: Crossroad, 1988, 65–98.

———— "Luther and the Unity of the Churches." *Church, Ecumenism & Politics. New Essays in Ecclesiology.* Trans. Robert Nowell. New York: Crossroad, 1988, 99–134. Another version in *Communio* 11 (1984), 210–226. Original: "Luther und die Einheit der Kirchen. Fragen an Joseph Kardinal Ratzinger." *Internationale katholische Zeitschrift* 12 (1983), 568–582.

Stransky, Tom and Hotchkin, John F., eds. *John Paul II: Addresses and Homilies on Ecumenism*, 1978–1980. Washington: USCC Publications, 1981.

Stransky, Tom and Sheerin, J., eds. *Doing the Truth in Charity: Statements of Popes Paul VI, John Paul I, John Paul II, and the Secretariat for Promoting Christian Unity, 1964–1980.* New York: Paulist Press, 1982.

Stransky, Tom. "Ecumenism (Unitatis Redintegratio)." *Modern Catholicism. Vatican II and After.* Ed. Adrian Hastings. New York: Oxford University Press, 1991, 113–117.

———— "The Secretariat for Promoting Christian Unity." *Modern Catholicism. Vatican II and After.* Ed. Adrian Hastings. New York: Oxford University Press, 1991, 182–184.

———— "World Council of Churches," *Dictionary of the*

Ecumenical Movement. Ed. Nicholas Lossky et al. Geneva: WCC, 1991, 1083–1090.

Stuhlmueller, Carroll, ed. *Women and Priesthood: future directions, a call to dialogue.* Collegeville: Liturgical Press, 1978.

Sullivan, Francis A. "'Subsistit In': The Significance of Vatican II's Decision to say of the Church of Christ not that it 'is' but that it 'subsists in' the Roman Catholic Church." *One in Christ* 22.2 (1986), 115–123.

Swidler, Leonard and Arlene Swidler, ed. *Women Priests: a Catholic commentary on the Vatican declaration.* New York: Paulist Press, 1977.

Tavard, George H. *A Review of Anglican Orders: the problem and the solution.* Collegeville: Liturgical, 1990.

———— *The Church, Community of Salvation. An Ecumenical Ecclesiology.* Collegeville: Liturgical Press, 1992.

———— "The Principles of an Ecumenical Opening." *Modern Catholicism. Vatican II and After.* Ed. Adrian Hastings. New York: Oxford University Press, 1991, 399–402.

Tillard, J.M.R. *The Bishop of Rome.* Trans. John de Satgé. Wilmington: Michael Glazier, 1983.

Together in Mission and Ministry. The Porvoo Common Statement with Essays on Church and Ministry in Northern Europe. London: Church House Publishing, 1993.

Tomkins, O.S., ed. *The Third World Conference on Faith and Order.* London: SCM, 1953.

"Toward Full Communion" and "Concordat of Agreement." Lutheran-Episcopal Dialogue, Series III. Ed. William A. Norgren and William G. Rusch. Minneapolis: Augsburg Fortress, 1991.

Walsh, James Joseph. *The Thirteenth, greatest of centuries.* 1907. New York: Catholic summer school press, 1913.

Witmer, Joseph W. and J. Robert Wright, ed. *Called to Full Unity: documents on Anglican-Roman Catholic relations 1966–1983.* Washington: United States Catholic Conference, 1986.

Wright, J. Robert. "Heritage and Vision: The Chicago-Lambeth Quadrilateral." *Quadrilateral at One Hundred. Essays on The Centenary of the Chicago-Lambeth Quadrilateral 1886/88—1986/88.* Ed. J. Robert Wright. Cincinnati: Forward Movement, 1988, 8–46.

Index